THE NEXT LEADER

DEVELOPING DISCIPLES TO BECOME LEADERS WITHIN THE CHURCH

FOREWORD BY: **JOHNNY M. HUNT**

STEPHEN D. OWENS

The Next Leader

ISBN-10: 0-9824622-7-1

ISBN-13: 978-0-9824622-7-0

Printed in the United States of America

Website: StephenOwens.org

Email: owensministry@gmail.com

ADVANCE PRAISE FOR THE NEXT LEADER

Physical and digital bookshelves are well-stocked with an excess of leadership books, some worth the read and some, well... not so much. My friend, Pastor Stephen Owensa, has produced a work that's worth picking up. The Next Leader is a thoughtful, biblical, historical, personal, practical, intentional, and inspirational offering on Christian leadership by a man who is humble yet hungry to develop and deploy leaders into Christ's harvest field.

Chad Allen,
Lead Pastor, Cuyahoga Valley Church

The Next Leader is an amazing work and will aid in the development of modern-day Christian leaders. This extraordinary author unveils the timeless principles of leadership through a patented examination of the biblical character John Mark. He skillfully blends together the voices of contemporary authors that prompts interactive leadership training, explores future opportunities, failures and fruitful progression as outgrowth of leadership development. This is a must read!

Rev. Dr. Gregory Walker,
Adjunct Professor Practical Theology,
Ashland University

Pastor Stephen Owens has done it again! Using John Mark's life as a case study, he reminds us of the way to *"find"* the next leader is to start with who we have. Using the *'next leader continuum,'* Owens shows how to begin with a disciple-making environment and lead disciples to become leaders. We understand, Jesus makes leaders, but we can position the church to see Him do what only He can do. As Barnabas did with John Mark, I am so thankful Jesus gives me a second chance! This is not a book to be read alone; get your leadership team together and work through the questions at the end of each chapter. Then, discover, develop, and deploy *the next leader!*

Steve Hopkins,
Bible Teaching/Leadership SCBO

The Next Leader is an insightful and personal look int the task of the church to equip the sains for ministry. Owens' words invite the reader into the task with excitement and practical applications. It is a helpful tool in the belt of the church.

Paul Morrison,
PhD., Director of Ohio Theological Institute

Pastor Stephen Owens has written a very timely book. As CEO of churchplanting.com, I interact with pastors and church leaders searching for their next pastor. What strikes me as odd is that these churches, many of which have a large membership base, are looking to find their next leader from outside of their current organization. The process for identifying, equipping, and releasing leaders is foundational to every organization. However, when it comes to ministry, the importance is amplified because people and their eternal destination are at stake. If you want to be more strategic and intentional about building a culture of leadership, this book is for you.

Dr. Jeffrey Hoglen,
D. Min., CEO Churchplanting.com

Pastor Stephen Owens continues his written legacy of leadership with a nuanced look at John Mark. Whether in the pulpit, pew, boardroom, or cubicle, Owens' leadership insights are relevant at church, work, or home. By analyzing John Mark's journey, Owens challenges the most likely, empowers the likely, and encourages the less likely to see leadership anew. Owens reminds us all that leadership is not reserved for the special few, but "The Next Leader" could be you!

Dr. Mark Louis Johnson Sr.,
Assistant Professor of Evangelism and Pastoral Ministry, New Orleans Baptist Theological Seminary

I highly recommend this book by my friend and brother Stephen Owens, The Next Leader. Great book for Pastors and an excellent study book for all church leaders. This book helps all leaders to re-think their mission and mandate within the local church to the body of Christ. A must have, a must read, and a must share.

Pastor Rodney Maiden,
Senior Pastor of Providence Baptist Church

I have read many books on leadership over my years in business and ministry. And have found this book to be one of the most practical, and actionable leadership books I've read in recent years. I have found that while many leadership books focus on basic principles and general ideas for leaders, very few dig deep into the biblical principles needed to effectively lead in ministry environments.

This is a book that anyone who aspires to lead in a ministry environment should read. The leadership principles are succinct, highly useful, and clearly biblical. The best part of this book is that every chapter concludes with practical exercises and strategies that can be applied to your daily leadership skills. It was quite a refreshing read. I highly recommend this book.

Josue Villa,
Station Manager, Moody Radio Cleveland

TABLE OF CONTENTS

FOREWORD

In the Next Leader Stephen Owens gives a case study of the life and leadership development of John Mark within the first century. The life of John Mark shows us how God can use some of the unlikeliest of individuals to impact the world for the glory of Jesus.

This book exposes the reader to the need for having a process in place to help new disciples grow into church leaders. The process Stephen uses and recommends is the "Next Leader Continuum". A crucial perspective in this process is every disciple has been called to make disciples.

The Next Leader deals with the importance of the local churches focusing on discipleship and leadership development. This is where the church concentrates of reaching people for Jesus, help those same individuals grow spiritually, and then developing as many disciples as possible into church leaders. An important step in their development is "intentional apprenticeship".

Within the pages of this book, you will be exposed to how failure and emotional health impacts leadership and what to do about it. The Next Leader is designed to help other pastors and church leaders think through and develop their process for developing future church leaders. Those of us within church leadership must continually look for the potential within all believers so we can assist them in becoming what God wants them to be.

Stephen isn't a theorist he's a pastor. From a pastoral perspective he shares his heart, his church's discipleship and leadership development processes, and his mishaps in pursuing this worthy goal of developing future church leaders.

I have found Stephen to be consumed with a passionate desire to develop leaders. This book can serve as a roadmap to growing disciples into fully devoted followers of Christ. Digest "The Next Leader" and then go develop leaders.

Johnny M. Hunt

Senior VP of Evangelism and Pastoral Leadership of NAMB

Pastor Emeritus of FBC Woodstock

Former President of SBC

INTRODUCTION

My hope is that this book can be a resource for the church of Jesus Christ and her leaders. I love the church (global and local) and truly believe that she is the only one who offers true hope (King Jesus and His Gospel) for the world. Because the church has this hope and it is so valuable, we must do what we can through the power of the Holy Spirit to reach people for Jesus, help those same individuals become more like Him, and help develop future leaders within the church.

For that to be done, the leaders within the local church must have a heart for God and a heart for people. Local church leaders have to place great emphasis on salvation, sanctification, and leadership development. Church leaders have to put processes in place to enable the local church to work on these important matters. I pray this book will help and encourage the church to do that.

This book is set up with blank spaces to answer questions that are presented in its pages. These blank spaces are found within the chapters as well as at the end of each chapter. There is also a note section at the end of each chapter for you to capture any thoughts you may have while reading and working through this book. I would also encourage you to use the margins within the book to write down ideas as they come to you. I hope as you read and write down your thoughts, the Spirit of the Lord will strengthen your resolve to be used by Him as the Lord builds His church. I pray the words of Mark 16:20 can be realized in our current generation, "And they went out and preached everywhere, the Lord working with them and confirming the word through the accompanying signs."

Pastor Stephen D. Owens

CHAPTER 1: WHO'S NEXT?

"A leader is one who knows the way, goes the way, and shows the way."

John Maxwell [1]

In the first century, close to the mid AD '40s, the church of Jesus Christ is crossing ethnic and city boundaries within the Roman Empire. Jews and Gentiles are hearing the Gospel of Jesus and many of them are believing the message and making Jesus their Lord. Because of this growth, the church has to raise up leaders from within the church to help new believers grow in their faith.

One church in particular where this is occurring is in the church in Antioch. Jews and Gentiles are worshiping together within this local church and they are seeking to live in unity in the midst of their diversity. When the church in Jerusalem hears about this church, they send one of their leaders, Barnabas, to see how things are going. When Barnabas arrives, he is overjoyed by what he is seeing God do; so he begins to teach about the importance of clinging to Christ together as a local fellowship of believers.

Not only does Barnabas stay in Antioch for a while teaching and encouraging the church, but he also finds a young man named Saul and brings him there to become a leader within this church. Barnabas does not stop with Saul. A few years later, while Barnabas and Saul are in Jerusalem dropping off an offering to the church from the Gentiles' churches across the Roman Empire, they pick up Barnabas's relative and bring him to Antioch with them. His name is John Mark.

John Mark is a young man who is open to adventure. He is willing to go to new places, learn new things, and willing to serve. Yet, at the same time, he has a lot of maturing to do when it comes to responsibility and commitment. At least that is how some folks view him. In particular, Saul could have viewed him that way because early on in their time of working together, John Mark left Barnabas and Saul while on a missionary journey. Saul had such a tainted view of John Mark's work ethic that he refused to do traveling missionary ministry with him anymore. This refusal by Saul brought Barnabas and Saul's ministry team to an end. It is Barnabas's choice to bring John Mark with him as he goes to check on churches.

Around AD 49, Barnabas and John Mark board a ship headed toward Cyprus to check on churches and do ministry among them. While they are on that ship, I can only imagine the thoughts going through John Mark's mind—such as: How Barnabas and Saul's ministry team broke up over him potentially coming with them; how adamant Saul was about not working with him; and what does it say about him, his reputation, and his future ministry if someone so important in the church saw him as not being fit for traveling ministry? Yet, John Mark is feeling some sense of optimism and hope because Barnabas stood up for him and chose to bring him along to do ministry.

What no one could have ever predicted, decades later, is that this young man would be a major catalyst within the church of Jesus Christ; that church history will tell us, "Apart from Thomas, Mark is likely the most widely traveled of all the apostles."[2] As well as, "The ancient tradition called Mark the universal apostle because he appears in all three known continents: Asia, Europe, and Africa. . . . Mark preached the same Gospel in all three continents."[3]

Nor would anyone have imagined that the Coptic Church in Egypt would boldly declare that their church tradition "is based on the teachings of Saint Mark,"[4] or that one of the church fathers, Cyprian, Bishop of Carthage, would "honor Mark as his predecessor."[5] No one would have ever predicted John Mark's story would turn out like this when he was entering that boat with Barnabas sailing toward Cyprus. How did this happen? As you read this book my hope is that you will see how God developed this amazing leader.

I pray, as you look at the life of John Mark and how God worked through him in lifting up the name of Jesus and expanding the Lord's church, that your passion for raising up new leaders will be set aflame. And if there is someone like John Mark in your church, that you will invest in developing him or her for a future in church leadership.

WHO IS THE NEXT LEADER IN YOUR CHURCH?

Can you identify anyone with potential to lead? In particular, can you identify anyone who can lead for the glory of Jesus Christ? Is there anyone in your sphere of influence that you can see leading in some capacity within your local church?

____

____

____

____

These are important and revealing questions. They are questions that the Barna Group and Pepperdine University in 2017 discussed concerning church leadership when they conducted their research on *The State of Pastors Report*. Their findings are quite interesting.

Under the Mentoring section, the report states, "The first step toward mentoring future leaders is finding them, and two out of three current pastors believe identifying suitable candidates is becoming more difficult."[6] The report goes on to highlight that 69% of pastors believe that it is becoming more difficult to identify suitable candidates.

That quote and statistic fascinated me; but a word in the quote sent my mind racing—*suitable*. I began to ask myself questions:

- What do they mean by suitable?
- Suitable to whom?
- Suitable by what standards?

A clue to the answer is given in the next sentence of the report. It gives us the percentage of pastors surveyed who agreed with the statement, "It's becoming harder to find mature young Christians who want to be pastors." Those who strongly agreed were 24% and those who somewhat agreed were 45%. This makes up the 69% of individuals who said, "It's becoming more difficult to identify suitable candidates." So, when leaders are saying "suitable," what they are really speaking of is "maturity" and "desire" (want to).

This revelation made me wonder, Are most leaders looking for people who are already mature before they will think about mentoring them? Now, I understand the concept of not placing a person in a major leadership role when he or she lacks maturity. The words of the Apostle Paul remind us of that when he tells Timothy, "A church leader must not be a new believer, because he might become proud, and the devil would cause him to fall" (1 Timothy 3:6).

But, if leaders are speaking about waiting to begin the conversation about leadership and mentorship until people are already mature, then I do not understand. If they were already mature, their need for a mentor would be greatly reduced. The need for mentorship is exponentially greater when people are novices and lacking in maturity.

There seems to be a disconnect between those looking for mentees and this current generation of young adults. In a more recent study entitled *The Connected Generation* released in 2019 by the Barna Group in partnership with World Vision, it captures the vantage point of committed followers of Jesus who are part of a local church from the ages of 18–35. A key finding in that report shows that one of the major experiences this age group is missing in the church is mentorship.[7]

Young adult Christians in this age range want to be mentored by those who are more mature, but those who are mature see them as immature; therefore, they will not enter into the mentorship and leadership conversation. However, the reality is that those who are 18–35 are immature because they haven't gone through the life experiences and training that their senior leaders have. As well, those within the younger age group are still trying to figure out who they are, what life is about, what leadership is, and if they are called to a leadership position. *The Connected Generation* report quotes David Kinnaman who says, "They (The Connected Generation) want the Church to be a laboratory of leadership, not just a place for spirituality."[8]

The desire part I understand, because you have to want to lead. As well, leaders should want to lead for the right reasons. Particularly, as a church leader you should want to lead so Jesus Christ can be glorified, and his name and fame can be known. Church leaders should want people to meet Jesus (salvation), and those who have met him to become like him (sanctification). Then, church leaders should help those believers become productive, visible representatives of the Lord Jesus in their communities to effect change for the glory of Christ and the betterment of society.

This isn't only for church leaders; this is also for Christians in leadership in the marketplace. I believe the above criteria applies for them as well. They, too, should want to see people come to know Christ and become more like him. Marketplace Christian leaders should desire to glorify Jesus, make disciples, and mentor the next generation, not only focus on creating quality products and growing the company's bottom line.

I believe the question—Can you identify anyone with the potential to lead others for the glory of Jesus?—is revealing. The answer we give says more about us and our leadership than it says about those whom God has sent us to lead. Whether you are in church leadership or marketplace leadership, if you can't see anyone with the potential to lead, there is something wrong with your sight.

The lens through which you view people may be tainted, darkened, or closed. If you want to know the lens you view people through, listen to your vocabulary. People have a tendency to think in extremes. On the negative end of the spectrum there may be statements like:

- These people are terrible.
- They can't do anything right, or without me.
- They are a bunch of dumb sheep.

Then in the polar opposite view, are statements about looking for the "best and the brightest," where leaders have more of a mentality of a talent scout than a developer of people. Leaders will say statements like:

- We want level 5 leaders.
- We are looking for high-capacity leaders.
- We want innovative and entrepreneurial leaders.

When I hear people say statements like that I always wonder, can you afford to pay those people—especially when it comes to churches and nonprofits? As well, what do you do with those people and leaders who are not level 5, high-capacity, and entrepreneurial individuals? The church has a responsibility to help them grow as well. Also, I wonder if the people who make statements like those above were the kind of people they are currently looking for when *they* entered into leadership?

When I look at my life, I would not have been considered the best and the brightest. My leadership journey began with barely graduating from high school, having comprehension problems, struggling to pronounce words, and being shy and timid. I was the person most leaders overlooked and still am. But I came to realize, by the grace of God, it's not how you begin that matters, it's how you finish that speaks the loudest.

When I started in leadership, I hated reading because I could barely do it. But with God's help, continuous learning, and pushing myself to read even when I didn't want to, my ability to comprehend grew and so did my communication skills. Now, I read at least one book a month, along with reading material for sermon and Bible study prep. And this book you are reading is my fifth published book.

It's not how you start; it's how you finish.

I'm looking for people who want to finish well.

I truly believe another major factor to my growth was God placing people in my life to affirm my gifts, potential, and taking multiple chances on me. God put men and women in my life who gave me opportunities to preach, teach, and lead. They allowed me to teach and lead a Sunday school class for close to 12 years before I began to pastor. Many of the individuals in my class were seniors and they allowed me to teach the lesson, even though they knew more than I did.

If any aspiring preachers are reading this book, please remember, don't despise the days of small beginnings. Don't despise teaching Sunday school and small Bible study classes. Develop your craft, learn how to teach, and how to answer questions.

I tell the ministers at the church I pastor, Mt. Calvary Baptist Church, if you can't teach when people can raise their hands and ask questions, you won't be able to preach effectively when people can't ask questions.

As leaders, if we aren't careful, we can stop taking risks on people. We can begin to look for "sure bets" and people who we think like us. This is especially true if you have been hurt and burnt multiple times before.

But we must remember, leadership is a risky business. It's risky because we are dealing with people and people can cause problems. People are also unpredictable and can be unreliable. Then, to top it off, people can be selfish and lack commitment. I'm not only talking about the people we lead, but us as leaders, too. We must continually remind ourselves that Jesus died and resurrected for people. Not our programs. Not our products. Not our equipment. Not our environments. He gave up his life for people.

So, leader, Jesus understands your role and that leadership is risky. He understands because he is leading us (leaders) and everyone who believes in him. He gave himself for us and he continually calls us to follow his leadership, even when we turn away from him. He is constantly calling us back to himself so we can walk with him.

Leaders, we must walk in our Master's footsteps and lead when it hurts and lead when people don't understand. Whether those people are members, volunteers, employees, or colleagues. Let's take a risk on people who Jesus died and resurrected for.

NOTES:

CHAPTER 2: RELATIONSHIPS MATTER

"The gospel flows best through the establishing of significant relationships that are authentic and healthy." [1]

Erwin Raphael McManus

"Now that's an amazing place." That's what I said to myself while I was watching the HULU television show *Broken Bread* with Roy Choi. He was interviewing Father Greg Boyle, founder of Homeboy Industries in Los Angeles, California. While Father Boyle was pastoring the Delores Mission back in 1992 in the projects of Los Angeles, he started a bakery (Homeboy Bakery) that focused on hiring gang members from rival gangs. While the government was focusing on locking gang members in jail, Father Boyle was focusing on showing a community love and a different way.

In 1992, Los Angeles was the gang capital of the US. Father Boyle and his parish were directly in the middle of the chaos. Father Boyle tells a story of how there was an abandoned bakery across the street from the church and they took a chance on opening the bakery to give gang members a job and skills training. In the midst of violence, retaliation, and imprisonment, Father Boyle focused on kinship, unconditional love, compassion, and inclusion.

Homeboy Industries helps gang members come out of the environment of gang life and puts them in an environment of productivity and respect, crossing lines to make friends out of old enemies. The Homies and Homegirls (program clients) go through an 18-month job-training program to prepare them for a career. They also offer services such as classes in anger management and parenting, counseling for mental health, as well as tattoo removal.

Each year Homeboy Industries helps over 10,000 gang members in L.A. alone. It "has evolved into the largest gang intervention, rehab, and re-entry program in the world."[2] Homeboy Industries is an amazing story of how a leader cared for those on the margins and created a counter-cultural community to help people change their lives.

In order to help people change their lives, it is important to expose them to a different kind of community with a different set of values so they can see what life can become. I believe this also applies to those who have become disciples of Jesus and possibly leaders in the Lord's church. In order to help them change for the glory of God, people need to be exposed to a counter-cultural community of believers who are living by a different set of values.

As we begin our journey to think through how to find the next leader, I think it's helpful for us to think through what I have called the Next Leader Continuum. The process looks like the diagram below. I came up with the process while the state of Ohio was in lockdown because of the COVID-19 stay-at-home order in 2020. I began thinking through how our own Mt. Calvary church can have more clarity on developing future leaders; and I believe the Next Leader Continuum will give us that clarity.

At Mt. Calvary we want to develop leaders for the purpose of making disciples of Jesus. To do that, we needed to create a leadership development process. The process is below.

Next Leader Continuum

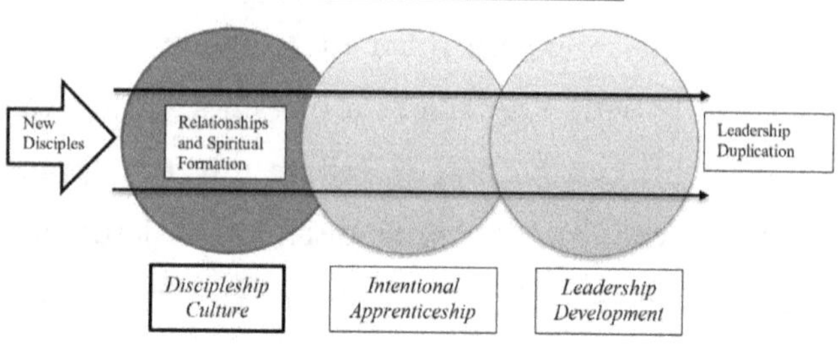

New disciples join a local church and become part of a discipleship culture. As those new disciples mature, they are encouraged to move into an intentional apprenticeship process so they can learn from other leaders within the church. While the leadership apprentices are continuing to grow as disciples of Jesus, they are also being challenged to develop as leaders. When they become leaders within the church, their learning and development continue so they can in turn have an apprentice, with the hope of developing future leaders so more disciples of Jesus can be made.

We will begin our examination of the life of John Mark by also looking at the discipleship culture he lived within. John (Yohanan) is his Hebrew name and Mark (Marcus) was his Roman name.[3] When I began to think about people in the Bible, on whom others took a risk in order to help them develop into leaders within the church, John Mark rose to the top. Initially,

John Mark would not have been considered a high-capacity leader. He would not have been the one the church members were whispering about concerning his great potential for church leadership.

When it comes to John Mark, there are usually two prominent moments people know about him. The first moment is located in Acts 13 when he left Paul and Barnabas in Pamphylia (modern day Turkey) when they went on their first missionary journey. The other aspect of his life that is known is that he wrote the Gospel of Mark, of which he received his information from the Apostle Peter. While there are some who push against this conclusion, most scholars do not.

In the introduction to the Gospel of Mark in the *Holman Study Bible,* NKJV Edition, it affirms the conclusion that John Mark received his information from the Apostle Peter. While the *Holman Study Bible* indicates the author of the Gospel of Mark is anonymous, it mentions the writing of Eusebius (AD 260–340) who was the Bishop of Caesarea in Asia Minor and a church historian. The passage says,

"Eusebius, the early church historian, writing in AD 326, preserved the words of Papias, an early church father. Papias quoted 'the elder,' probably John, as saying that Mark recorded Peter's preaching about the things Jesus said and did, but not in chronological order. Thus, Mark was considered the author of this Gospel even in the first century."[4]

Therefore, most scholars agree that Mark's writing was the first Gospel account written, around early AD 50. His account became something of a reference guide for Matthew (mid to late 50s) and also Luke (late 50s, early 60s). *The Holman Study Bible* confirms this when it says, "Most Bible scholars are convinced that Mark was the earliest Gospel and served as one of the sources for Matthew and Luke."[5] Now how on God's green earth did he go from walking out on a job assignment, to being able to write one of the four Gospel narratives about the Lord Jesus?

WHO IS JOHN MARK?

When we go to the Bible, there isn't any information concerning John Mark's nationality and childhood. However, many scholars have declared him to be from the area of Palestine. Dr. Thomas C. Oden indicates in his book *The African Memory of Mark* that a different narrative is communicated on the continent of Africa. He writes, "John Mark, according to these traditions (African), came from and returned to Africa to become the first person sent by

Jesus's followers to teach firsthand about Christianity on the African continent."[6]

When people in the Western world hear this, it is somewhat jarring to them. Reason being, as Dr. Oden puts it, "Western scholars have tended to treat Mark as one who shows up frequently throughout the New Testament but is probably Palestinian in origin, and almost never regarded as African. The problem: African popular memory of Mark is very different from the Western memory." He goes on to say, "The African narrative is often pigeonholed as unsupported by reliable textual evidence and thought to be naïve, since accompanied by miracles, dreams, and visions."[7]

While there are different views on the nationality of John Mark, there is a possibility that he could have been an African Jew. We know this is possible because from Scripture there were Jews on the continent of Africa. As a matter of fact, there were African Jews in Jerusalem on the day of Pentecost in Acts chapter two. Acts 2:20 lets us know there were Jews from Egypt, Libya, and Cyrene in Jerusalem on the day of Pentecost. All three areas are on the continent of Africa. While we cannot say for certain where John Mark was from, because Scripture does not tell us, let us not exclude the possibility of Africa.

The first time we encounter John Mark's name is in Acts 12. The Apostle James, the Apostle John's brother, one of the "sons of thunder," has already been martyred. The Apostle Peter was in jail, but an angel frees him from prison.

When the Apostle Peter realized that his release from jail was not a dream, he went to a house in Jerusalem where a prayer meeting was occurring. The people in the house were praying for Peter.

A sidenote here, we must pray for our leaders and not only those within the church. All leaders need prayer, like every other person in the world. We know this to be true because the Bible affirms it. 1 Timothy 2:1-2 tells us, "Therefore I exhort first of all the supplications, prayer, intercessions, and giving of thanks be made for all men, for kings and all who are in authority, that we may lead a quiet and peaceable life in all godliness and reverence."

In verse 12, we are told whose house Peter went to; it was "the house of Mary, the mother of John whose surname was Mark." *The New Interpreter's Bible* makes a comment about Mary that's rather interesting. It says, "She is apparently an independent woman and is sufficiently wealthy to employ a maidservant."[8] In verse 13 we are given the name of the maidservant, Rhoda.

The Bible does not give us any details about who John Mark's father was. More than likely he was dead during the time of the book of Acts. There is very little recorded and written in western culture concerning John Mark's father. Dr. Thomas C. Oden does a deep dive into the life and legacy of John Mark in *The African Memory of Mark* where he gives research on who John Mark's father could have been.

As it relates to his mother Mary and her home, F.F. Bruce says in his commentary in *The Book of the Acts,* that Mary's house was "one of the chief meeting-places of Jerusalem."[9] Her house was large enough that the early church could go there and gather for prayer. *The Life Application Commentary* brings up the possibility that Mary's "house may have been the location of Jesus's last supper with his disciples (Luke 22:8) and/ or the place where the 120 earliest believers met for prayer (Acts 1:15; 2:1)."[10] While this is not detailed in the Scriptures, it is an interesting thought.

F.F. Bruce wrote in another one of his works, *The Pauline Circle*, "Mary, owned a house in Jerusalem which served as a meeting place for one group of the primitive church in that city—an influential group, for Peter evidently belonged to it."[11] So this would mean, "Mark grew up, then, in close contact with the earliest leaders of the church."[12] He would have heard and seen the apostles preach and teach. He would have observed and experienced their leadership, encouragement, and the making of disciples within the early church. He would have spent time with them and talked with them.

DISCIPLESHIP ENVIRONMENT

Exposure to leadership is important. Emerging leaders being around positional leaders allows relationships to form and grow. And those relationships expose emerging leaders to the challenges of leadership. Emerging leaders also gain the privilege of gleaning from positional leaders' knowledge, wisdom, and experience. It is of crucial importance that church members get to know the leaders in the church. That is how relationships are formed and exposure can begin.

John Mark's relationship with early church leaders was formed in the context of community. It was developed in an environment (or culture) where not only were relationships important, but spiritual transformation was important too. I would venture to say that Mark's early Christian development was cultivated in an atmosphere of discipleship. Discipleship is foundational for leadership. People must be disciples of Jesus before they are leaders in his church. The maxim must be discipleship before leadership.

In the book *Building Leaders*, Aubrey Malphurs and Will Mancini deal with this essential connection of discipleship and leadership. They write,

> Thus leadership builds on discipleship. It's not only foundational but also imperative that a ministry develop its potential leaders as disciples; otherwise, they will find it most difficult to function well as leaders in the church. Leaders must be growing disciples. However, as disciples are developed, they must receive training in leadership so they can be good leaders.[13]

To develop potential leaders, current leaders must focus on making disciples first, then on developing future leaders. Malphurs and Mancini go on to say, "Ultimately the reason we build leaders is to make disciples, but the processes are distant, with leadership building subordinate to disciple making . . . Leaders . . . are not the final 'product' of the church, disciples are. Leaders simply help the church make more mature disciples. Leaders train leaders so that more disciples can be produced."[14]

I would agree with their assessment of the church's objective. Our focus is not to make leaders, but disciples—even though leadership is crucial within the church of Jesus. Since that is the case, leaders who desire to make leaders must focus on making disciples of Jesus Christ. I believe this is shown in the life of John Mark. John Mark became a follower of Jesus first, then he became a leader in the church. Some believe the Apostle Peter was more than likely the one to lead him to faith in Jesus (1 Peter 4).

John Mark's faith was cultivated in the environment of first-century church discipleship. We see at Mary's house, John Mark's mother, that they were in the midst of prayer when the Apostle Peter arrives. This scene gives us a glimpse into the corporate discipleship practices of the early church. They assembled for corporate prayer. Congregational prayer is one of the practices of the early church.

To find out more about the early church's discipleship process we can look at Acts 2:42-47:

> And they continued steadfastly in the apostles' doctrine and fellowship, in the breaking of bread, and in prayers. Then fear came upon every soul, and many wonders and signs were done through

> the apostles. Now all who believed were together, and had all things in common, and sold their possessions and goods, and divided them among all, as anyone had need. So continuing daily with one accord in the temple, and breaking bread from house to house, they ate their food with gladness and simplicity of heart, praising God and having favor with all the people. And the Lord added to the church daily those who were being saved.

If we look carefully at what is being described, we can see how the early church made disciples. We see their practices, environments, and fruit.

<u>Spiritual Practice/Disciplines:</u>

- Steadfast in apostles' doctrine: biblical knowledge (teaching and learning)
- Fellowship: being together in growing relationships
- Breaking bread: communion and regular meals
- Prayer: talking to God together
- Sold possessions: sacrifice
- Divided among all: generosity
- Among any who had need: serving

Spiritual Environments:

- Temple meeting: large gathering (like worship services)
- House to house: small gathering (like Bible study groups)

Spiritual Fruit:

- Gladness: joy
- Fear: reverence of God
- Wonders/signs: the power of God
- Praising God: celebrating and thanking God
- Adding to the church: salvation of new disciples of Jesus

As we think about disciple making, we need to begin to think through the same categories.

1. What spiritual disciplines should disciples of Jesus practice?

___

___

___

2. What environments should disciples participate in?

___

___

___

3. What spiritual fruit or results should disciples show in their lives?

___

___

___

We must think through these questions, because as Ed Stetzer and Daniel Im said in *Planting Missional Churches*, "Disciple development occurs through the right environments, content, and opportunities in which individuals consistently grow toward spiritual maturity. Discipleship does not happen by accident."[15]

They go on to write,

> By definition a disciple is a follower of Christ. A disciple is a learner. A disciple is also a believer who practices biblical habits that enable him or her to live the Christian life effectively. A mature believer displays many behaviors or habits such as prayer, evangelism, Bible study, and fasting. The disciple must intentionally practice these habits in order to develop effectively as a disciple.[16]

The book that revolutionized my understanding of disciple making as a local church was *Simple Church* by Thom Rainer and Eric Geiger. This book helped me understand that not only is spiritual growth a process, but it's also done best when leaders work through how they will work with God to make disciples. I recommend *Simple Church* to any leader searching to find out how to make disciples as a community of believers.

Simple Church walks you through the importance of having a clear discipleship process that allows disciples to see their next steps in their spiritual walk so they can become more like Jesus. While *Simple Church* helped me to grasp the concept of communal discipleship and to begin to work out the initiated framework of our process, it was the Church of the Highlands in Alabama that opened up the hood of their church at their GROW conference and showed me how it played out in everyday life.

Seeing how the Church of the Highlands operated was eye opening and inspiring. They taught about their ministry model and their Growth Track. And to a degree, our discipleship model and new member assimilation process is patterned after theirs, along with some principles from Ranier and Geiger's *Simple Church* and Will Mancini's *Church Unique*.

People need a process to go through, to help them grow as disciples. When we think about it, we realize that spiritual transformation and formation is a process. In theological terms, it's called Sanctification. In *Kingdom First* by Jeff Christopherson and Mac Lake they write, "Without some kind of process, people generally fall through the discipleship cracks. The elements involved in a discipleship process are actually a strategic attempt to create environments where God makes disciples who live daily with Jesus."[17]

Some folks will also call this your assimilation process. It's generally a combination of classes and environments. At Mt. Calvary, we have new member classes which we call the Growth Track, which are borrowed from the Church of the Highlands. While there are other ministry models and processes in the global church, this is the one the Lord led us to use at Mt. Calvary. (See *Simple Church* by Thom Rainer and Eric Geiger and *Planting Missional Churches* by Ed Stetzer and Daniel Im for more models and processes.)

OUR PROCESS

To help me teach our model and philosophy, I use FIVE questions.

1. **What KIND of disciples are we making?**

It's shown in our **Mission**: *Make disciples of Jesus Christ who love God and people.*

This is based on the Great Commandment and the Great Commission.

- The Great Commandment is Matthew 22:38-40:

  "Jesus replied, 'You must love the Lord your God with all your heart, all your soul, and all your mind.' This is the first and greatest commandment. A second is equally important: 'Love your neighbor as yourself.' The entire law and all the demands of the prophets are based on these two commandments." (NLT)

- The Great Commission is Matthew 28:18-20:

  "Therefore, go and make disciples of all the nations, baptizing them in the name of the Father and the Son and the Holy Spirit. Teach these new disciples to obey all the commands I have given you. And be sure of this: I am with you always, even to the end of the age." (NLT)

2. **How do we TELL disciples who we are and what we do?**

This is done through our **Growth Track**. Our Growth Track is comprised of five, one-and-a-half-hour classes.

- *Church 101:* In this class we focus on Mt. Calvary's DNA. The class exposes new believers to our mission, vision, and ministry philosophy. The class also makes sure the new member is led through the plan of Salvation (using the Romans Road process). We also talk about baptism, communion, stewardship, and our membership covenant.
- *Essentials 201:* This class focuses on learning spiritual habits so disciples can grow. We go more in depth on the teaching of salvation as well as the importance of Bible reading, prayer, community, relying on the Holy Spirit, and generosity.
- *Discovery 301:* This class deals with discovering how God has uniquely created the disciple. We talk about the importance of serving, the gifts of the Spirit, and different ministry opportunities in our church.
- *Mission 401:* This class centers on how to share Jesus's story (Gospel) and the disciple's story (testimony). It's important that disciples know the Gospel of Jesus and how to share it. Also, we want them to understand the

importance of their salvation story and how to share that, as well.

- *Leadership 501:* This class is an introduction to leadership within Mt. Calvary. Disciples are exposed to what leadership looks like for us at Mt. Calvary. They are informed about what traits we are looking for in leaders and the responsibilities they will have as leaders with our church. They are also exposed to a more in-depth understanding of our ministry philosophy and our leadership apprentice process.

3. **Where do disciples GO to grow?**

This is our **Discipleship Process** (Strategy). In our process, we encourage believers to participate in five environments to help them grow. We call our environments "steps." In these steps, disciples are encouraged to grow in their walk with Christ.

- *Worship services:* This is where we are celebrating Christ in communal worship and biblical preaching with other believers and those looking to find out more about Christ.
- *Small-group* Bible *studies:* This is where disciples are able to grow in relationship with other disciples, while growing in their relationship with Christ, by studying the Bible.

- *Ministry Teams:* At this step, disciples are using their gifts and talents in the local church to serve other believers and those who visit our church.
- *Outreach and evangelism:* This is an opportunity for disciples to serve in our community, to show the love of Jesus Christ while looking for an opportunity to share the Gospel of Jesus.
- *Leadership Gathering:* We have ongoing leadership training and development for potential and existing leaders at Mt. Calvary.

One of our goals is to have 80% participation in our discipleship process. We desire to flip the 80-20 principle around. While we are not there yet, we are striving for it. This will reduce ministry burnout and spread the work of the ministry out among more church members, thereby creating more ownership and buy-in with the members of our church.

4. **What do we want disciples to FEEL?** (individually and collectively)

These are our **Values** as a local congregation. They are connected to our Discipleship Process (steps). These are the things we hope people sense and feel when they interact with members of our church.

- Loving God
- Connecting with each other (to the church)
- Serving people
- Reaching a diverse world
- Leading others
- Pursuing Excellence (Continual Improvement)
- Healthy disciple-making church

These values can also translate into how a disciple lives life outside of the church community. For example:

- People who come in contact with them are able to see they love God.
- They are connecting with other Christians, even if they are of other denominations and traditions.
- They are serving people in their sphere of influence in a Christlike manner.
- They are reaching anyone and everyone they can for Jesus—with the Gospel of Jesus.
- They are leading others by being a model for them to follow at work and in their community.

- They are continuing to get better in what they do for the glory of God.

5. **What do we want a disciple to BECOME?**

This is the **Fruit** we are looking for in disciples. (In *Church Unique* by Will Mancini, these are called "marks.") From our discipleship process, we are hoping disciples produce five traits in their lives. When church leaders see disciples displaying these traits, they can gauge the growth of the disciples and if the culture we are trying to produce is operating well. The traits are:

- *Learners (learning):* Regularly self-feeding in the Bible.
- *Friends (befriending):* Fellowshipping with other believers.
- *Gardeners (gardening):* Growing (Conforming to) in biblical behavior.
- *Servants (serving):* Helping and serving people.
- *Witnesses (witnessing):* Telling people about Jesus and what He has done in their lives.

YOUR PROCESS

Leader, does your church have a process in place to makedisciples?____________________________

We cannot focus on developing leaders until we focus on making disciples. The purpose of leadership development within the church is to make sure we are able to make more disciples of Christ who are maturing in their faith.

We have learned the grease that helps people move more easily through the discipleship process is relationship. People don't only want to attend a friendly church, they want to make friends at church. You must have people in the process reaching out and building relationships with other disciples and encouraging them to take the next step. It doesn't matter who the person is. It can be a leader, teacher, friend, or just someone else in the church who knows and believes in the process, and is committed to how your local church makes disciples.

As you begin to think through your church's spiritual formation and discipleship process, it's helpful to think through eight essential attributes Lifeway Research observed through their Transformational Discipleship Assessment ©. Lifeway Research found that "highly effective disciples" have eight attributes in common. [18]

1. Bible Engagement
2. Obeying God and Denying Self
3. Serving God and Others
4. Sharing Christ
5. Exercising Faith
6. Seeking God
7. Building Relationships
8. Unashamed Transparency

For more details, please refer to *Planting Missional Churches* by Stetzer and Im.

I think a good quote to leave this chapter is from the book *Kingdom First* by Christopherson and Lake. We must remember, "Only God can make disciples. But He uses our intentionality as a platform to do what only He can do."[19]

EXERCISE:

1. What KIND of disciples are you making?

___

___

___

2. How do you TELL disciples who you are and what you do?

___

___

___

3. Where do disciples GO to grow?

___

___

___

4. What do you want disciples to FEEL?

___

___

___

5. What do you want disciples to BECOME?

___

___

___

NOTES:

CHAPTER 3: EXPOSURE TO OPPORTUNITY

"For it seemed good to the Holy Spirit and to us to lay upon you no greater burden than these essentials"

Acts 15:28 (NASB)

"That's where I got started in the animation business."[1] This is what Walt Disney said when he told the story of his life. He was speaking of the time he was hired at the Kansas City Film Ad Company in 1920. It was there Disney was exposed to the industry of animation. Not only was he exposed to the industry, he learned the craft of animation. This put him on the trajectory to where he would eventually create Disney Studios.

During this time, Disney was already an entrepreneur. He and his friend Ubbe Iwerks were already in business together. They formed Iwerks-Disney Commercial Artists in Kansas City,

Missouri.[2] While the company did not last long, Disney's fire for entrepreneurship was already kindling. Also, during his time at Kansas City Film Ad Company, Walt Disney worked at nighttime experimenting with The Universal (motion picture camera) and making "theatrical cartoons." He made a set of cartoons called the Newman Laugh-O-Grams that he tried to sell to a small theater chain called Newman Theaters. In 1922, Disney left the Kansas City Film Ad Company and started Laugh-O-Gram Studios with Ubbe Iwerk.[3]

From the beginning, the company had cashflow problems, but it was able to stay afloat by doing some advertisements for local businesses. This is also the time Disney came up with the idea for a series of cartoons called Alice in Cartoonland which began to get some traction. Unfortunately, Laugh-O-Gram Studios eventually failed, and Walt Disney moved to California. When Disney remembers this time in his life, he makes a great statement; he said, "I'd failed, but I learned a lot out of that. I think it's important to have a good hard failure when you're young."[4]

Walt Disney failed getting two companies off the ground before starting a business that flourished. Yet in the midst of his failures, he continued to expose himself to new ideas and to try new artistry techniques. The exposure Disney encountered was extremely important. You don't know what you don't know until you have been exposed to it. Disney may have never moved into the direction of animation if he had not been exposed to it at Kansas City Film Ad Company. That job was a great opportunity for him to learn. Let's begin to think through how we can expose disciples to the role of leadership.

APPRENTICESHIP

If we are serious about helping disciples becomes leaders in the church, we must expose them to the ministry of leadership. One way to do that is to encourage people to move into an apprenticeship process, which is the next phase that is highlighted on the Next Leader Continuum. This phase can feel subjective at times. The length of the phase depends on the maturity level of the disciples when they enter apprenticeship—as well as their faithfulness and growth while they are in the process.

Next Leader Continuum

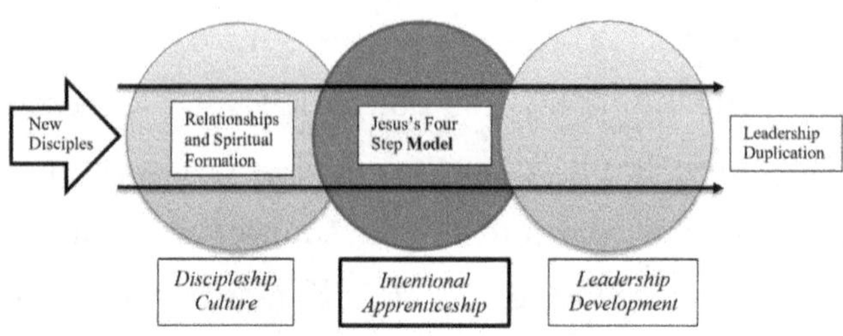

When I became the Pastor of Mt. Calvary in 2014, I added the apprentice position to our church. I began to understand the importance of this position while I was doing research to start a local church called Triumphant Assembly four years earlier. Triumphant Assembly merged with Mt. Calvary when I became the pastor. The apprentice process made sense to me in developing new leaders. One of the phrases I say all the time is, if you can't follow well, you will not lead well. The apprentice process helps people become more serious about following, because they know they will become leaders with people following them.

Even though I instituted the apprentice position over five years ago, we have been working out the kinks in the process. We have not done the process flawlessly, and we are still trying to improve it. We want to be intentional in our process of developing apprentice leaders. We use the word intentional because the apprenticeship process has to be purposeful and strategic. The process should be designed in such a way that it helps transition disciples into leaders. I would venture to say we were intentional in adding apprenticeship into the church, but not intentional in how it was going to operate and move people through the process. In this chapter you will see some of our process and our mistakes in our commitment to develop emerging leaders.

Ram Charan writes in his book *Leaders at All Levels* about the importance and value of apprenticeship. Charan writes, "Apprenticeship is at the heart of this new approach to leadership development. To understand why, you'll have to come to grips with a potentially controversial belief: leadership can only be developed through practice. Those who have talent for leadership must develop their abilities by practicing in the real world and converting that experience into improved skill and judgment. That conversion does not take place in a classroom."[5]

Apprenticeship allows emerging leaders to gain real-world experience under the watchful eye of an experienced leader. The apprentice is able to develop competencies and practice leadership skills in an environment that allows him or her to make mistakes while developing.

When we look at the life of John Mark, I believe the process of Intentional Apprenticeship is clearly seen. John Mark jumps back into the story in Acts, at the end of chapter 12, with Barnabas and Saul. Dr. Luke records in verse 25, "And Barnabas and Saul returned from Jerusalem when they had fulfilled their ministry, and they also took with them John whose surname was Mark."

BACKGROUND CHECK

Before we dive into verse 25, I believe it would be time well spent to learn a little about Barnabas and Saul. The Scripture tells us in Acts 4:36 that Barnabas's official name was Joses. The apostles gave him the name Barnabas because he was a person of great encouragement. He was a person of influence, since he was a part of the Levitical Priesthood. The Scripture says he was "a Levite of the country of Cyprus" (Acts 4:36). He was also, more than likely, a person of means because he sold a piece of land and gave the proceeds to the church.

Initially, Saul was a Pharisee who persecuted the church of Jesus. The first time he is mentioned in Scripture, he is holding the coats of the people stoning Deacon Stephen in Acts 7:58. Then in chapter eight he received authorization to throw Christians in prison. In chapter nine, Saul had an amazing encounter with the Risen Jesus and he received Jesus as Lord. After this encounter, he spends some time in Damascus, Arabia (Gal. 1:17), and Jerusalem.

The Scripture tells us in Acts 9:27 that while in Jerusalem, "Barnabas took him (Saul) and brought him to the apostles. And he declared to them how he had seen the Lord on the road, and that he had spoken to him, and how he had preached boldly at Damascus in the name of Jesus." After leaving Jerusalem, Saul returns to his hometown of Tarsus until Barnabas comes to get him in Acts 11:25 to bring him to the church in Antioch to serve in leadership with him. As we see from this experience with Saul, Barnabas is willing to take a risk on risky individuals. Taking a risk on people was a part of his leadership style. Then in Acts 12 they deliver an offering to the church in Jerusalem from the church in Antioch.

ENTER JOHN MARK

While we do not know the exact date when John Mark went with Barnabas and Saul, F.F. Bruce gives wise counsel when he writes, "Barnabas and Paul probably did not set out for Jerusalem until sometime after Agrippa's death."[6] Dr. Warren Wiersbe writes in his Bible Commentary about Herod Agrippa's death, "Herod contracted some affliction in his bowels and died five days later, according to Josephus. This was in AD 44."[7] F.F. Bruce states, "Whereas Agrippa died in A.D. 44, a probable date for the famine-relief visit of Barnabas and Paul is A.D. 46."[8]

This is a good moment for another side note. Churches, we must help one another. We are on the same team. We are all waiving the blood-stained banner. Jesus is OUR King. Too many times we find church leaders only concerned about themselves and their ministry while a church down the street is struggling. Leaders, we should help and encourage one another.

Some speculate that Barnabas and Saul could have stayed at Mary's house while in Jerusalem.[9] We find out from the book of Colossians that Barnabas was John Mark's cousin. F.F. Bruce indicates that Wycliffe confirmed Barnabas and John Mark were cousins in his translation. He writes, "Wycliffe had given the correct rendering 'cousin' (following the Latin *consobrinus).*" Bruce goes on to write, "There is no ambiguity about the Greek word *anepsios*, which Paul uses. 'Cousin'—even 'first cousin'—is what it means."[10]

This information allows us to go a little deeper in the life of John Mark and to see his life from a different perspective. Not only was he around influential church leaders in Jerusalem, such as Apostle Peter, but now we see he is also related to an influential leader, Barnabas, who used to be a Levite.

This could possibly mean that John Mark was also of the Levitical priesthood. Thomas Oden brings up this same idea when he mentions the preface of the Gospel of Mark in the Vulgate. He writes, "From an early tradition, the Vulgate preface to Mark's Gospel assumed that Mark himself was a Jewish priest: 'Mark the Evangelist, who exercised the priestly office in Israel, a Levite by race.' "[11]

ANTIOCH EXPERIENCE

We find out in chapter 13 when the trio left Jerusalem, that Barnabas and Saul took John Mark to the church in Antioch. The city of Antioch was about 300 miles away from Jerusalem. Antioch was an amazing city within the Roman Empire.

Dr. Jeff Iorg gives us great detail about this city in his book *The Case for Antioch*. He begins his description of the city by writing, "Antioch was a large, complex, pluralistic, multicultural city."[12] He goes on to write,

> What was Antioch like? It was the third largest city in the Roman Empire with a population estimated between 500,000 and 800,000. . . . It was a beautiful city laid out in a grid pattern with streets positioned to take advantage of cool afternoon breezes. It was located near the mouth of the Orontes River, about fifteen miles from its port city of Seleucus, making Antioch both an inland city and a major seaport. The location is now Antakya, Turkey, about twelve miles from the Syrian border.[13]

Not only was Antioch a prominent city within the Roman empire, as Iorg indicates, "Antioch was infamous for its religious practices."[14] It was a "cosmopolitan city of religious pluralism worshiping a pantheon of gods and goddesses."[15] He goes on to say about Antioch, it "was also a multicultural stewpot. Greeks, Syrians, Phoenicians, Jews, Arabs, Persians, and Italians were all part of this city's population mix." He concludes his description of Antioch by comparing it to major cities of the world. He says, "In that regard Antioch was a lot like San Francisco, Rio de Janeiro, Paris, or Cairo."[16]

Barnabas and Paul took John Mark to this magnificent city to do ministry with them. This would have been an amazing opportunity for John Mark. Emerging leaders, be careful not to waste the opportunities the Lord gives you to learn and be used by him.

CHURCH HERITAGE

This willingness to bring John Mark with them is grounded in the early church discipleship culture. The early church has a heritage of apprenticeship going back to Jesus himself. The application of apprenticeship is clearly seen in the ministry of Jesus. The Gospels show us that Jesus operated on the Rabbi/disciple model (apprenticeship). The way he acquired his initial disciples is quite revealing to how the early church transitioned disciples into leaders.

Dave Ferguson and Jon Ferguson detail the simple apprenticeship process Jesus used during his ministry in their book *Exponential.* They observe Jesus's model in Mark 3:13-15. They see the process as follows:

- *Apprentice selection:* Jesus picked people "he wanted" (v.13). Jesus's selection for apprenticeship was a relational process; he selected people he wanted around him.
- *Apprentice expectation:* Jesus "designate[d] them apostles" (v.14). Apostle means "sent one." Jesus was clear from the beginning that

his expectation of an apprentice was that he or she would be sent out on mission.

- *Apprentice preparation:* Jesus's disciples were "with him" (v.14). The primary means of training and developing these world changers was life-on-life relationships. Being with Jesus was their preparation.
- *Apprentice graduation:* Jesus concluded their apprenticeship by "send[ing] them out to preach and to have authority to drive out demons" (vv.14-15). The apprenticeship concluded when they could do what Jesus did.[17]

As leaders, we must figure out a way to help disciples develop into leaders. It does not really matter what we call the process. It can be apprenticeship, training, mentoring, etc. The real concern is: do we have an intentional process that moves God's people toward leadership?

SIMPLE APPRENTICESHIP

We see this intentional process in John Mark as he followed Barnabas and Paul. Let's look at the first two components now and return to discuss the last two later in the chapter.

Selection:

We are not sure how the selection process went for them in selecting John Mark to follow them. We are not informed on why they allowed him to come with them. It's possible it was because of Barnabas's and John Mark's family ties, or it could have been they saw promising quality. Or, they wanted to expose him to a new church. Or, they just wanted to raise up leaders, so they took a risk on him. We don't know why they selected him, but they did.

When we select apprentices at Mt. Calvary, we want to make sure they have completed our Growth Track before moving them into the apprenticeship process. We also want them to be participating in our Discipleship process where they are faithfully serving in ministry, consistently attending worship services, and participating in a small-group Bible study.

We encourage the mentoring ministry leaders of the future apprentices to answer the 4 "C" evaluation questions before they enter into an apprenticeship relationship. I was exposed to these 4 "Cs" in a pastor training session with Dr. R. A. Vernon at his conference, *The Gathering of the Shepherds Conference*. Preferably, the future apprentices are already serving in ministry with the leader so the leader can answer the questions as easily as possible. These questions have been added to our leadership team toolkit over time. As I have been working with the leaders at Mt. Calvary in helping them develop apprentices, I began to share with them the questions I ask myself when I look for leaders. Our leaders need to have a grid of questions to ask themselves as they look for apprentices:

- Competence: Can they do the work?
- Character: Are they growing as Christians? How do they treat people?
- Chemistry: Would you and the prospective apprentices work well together?
- Culture: Do they fit the leadership culture of the church?

Expectation:

We aren't privy to Barnabas's and Paul's expectations for John Mark during the apprenticeship process. We find out later that Barnabas and Paul each had a different set of expectations for John Mark when they attempt to go on their second missionary journey. We also don't know what they expected him to learn and experience during his time of apprenticeship. But we do know what he experienced: a new church, a multi-ethnic church, a new culture, how they made disciples at Antioch, and a diverse leadership community within the church.

In order for apprentices to get the most out of your apprenticeship processes, you must have clear expectations for them during their apprenticeship. There should be a plan in place beforehand. You should ask questions such as:

- What do we want apprentices to learn? The leader has to figure out what it takes to run the ministry well. This has to do with the competence you want apprentices to learn—helping them learn to lead.

___

___

- What do we want apprentices to experience? The leader has to know the specific environments you want apprentices to be involved in—exposure to situations.

___

___

- What do we want apprentices to do during the apprenticeship? The leader must know the specific tasks and responsibilities you want the apprentices to complete—accomplishments help build confidence.

___

___

- What is the end result of the apprenticeship? The leader needs to know what fruit he or she desires to see in the lives of the apprentices when the apprenticeship is over—what kind of growth they have each experienced as a person, a disciple, and a leader.

At Mt. Calvary, our expectations for apprentices are that they are willing to:

- Learn how to be Christian leaders.
- Support their ministry team leaders.
- Serve their ministry team members.
- Take responsibility when it is delegated to them.
- Lead when given the opportunity.

We also want them to develop seven leadership qualities during their apprenticeship. These qualities aren't original to us. We got them from John Maxwell's book *Developing the Leader Within*.

- *Integrity*: Be authentic. Your words should match your actions.
- *Priorities*: Think ahead and prioritize

responsibilities. Know what's important and do those things. Delegate the rest.

- *Problem-Solving*: Don't complain about what's wrong. Give suggestions on how to make things work better.
- *Attitude*: Have the disposition (mindset) of possibility and positivity. Believe that God is able to do anything. We must have faith and be willing to work with him.
- *People*: Understand that people are more important than tasks and systems. Jesus died and resurrected for people not things.
- *Vision*: Have an image of the kind of leader you want to be. The greatest leader in the world is Jesus and we should aspire to be like him and lead like him.
- *Self-Discipline*: Be able to control your temper and practice biblical restraint.

During their apprenticeship there are additional behaviors we want our apprentices to practice:

- Encourage others to go through our Growth Track and Discipleship process.
- Learn our church culture.

- Grow as disciples of Jesus.
- Become leaders who make disciples of Jesus who love God and people.

Create an Apprentice Position Description:

For clarity's sake, I believe it's helpful for the ministry leaders to write up an apprentice position description so apprentices can know specifically how they will serve and what is expected of them in that ministry role. This is something I learned over time. The leader of each ministry should work on creating this because he or she knows what's needed to make sure the ministry runs well. The leaders should work with senior leadership within the church, to reduce misunderstanding and so everyone is on the same page as it relates to mission, vision, and the core values of the church.

BACK TO ANTIOCH

The church in Antioch was an urban, cutting-edge, multiethnic community of Jew and Gentile believers. As well, it was a church-planting church. They sent out missionaries to start new Gospel works around the Roman Empire. We find out from Dr. Luke in chapter 11 of the Book of Acts, that this church was started with a different ministry philosophy than other churches during that time.

We are told in Acts 11:19-21, "Now those who scattered after the persecution that arose over Stephen traveled as far as Phoenicia, Cyprus, and Antioch, preaching the word to no one but the Jews only. But some of them were men of Cyprus and Cyrene, who, when they had come to Antioch, spoke to the Hellenist, preaching the Lord Jesus. And the hand of the Lord was with them, and a great number believed and turned to the Lord."

As a side note, I find it interesting that Dr. Oden says in *The African Memory of Mark* that a part of African tradition indicates that John Mark was a part of a "Jewish family of Cyrene."[18] And Barnabas was from the island of Cyprus. The disciples who planted the multiethnic church in Antioch were from these two cities as well. While there is no indication that Barnabas and John Mark knew these men or had any connection with them, it is an interesting thought, at least to me.

The Bible also allows us to see the leadership team in Antioch. Acts 13:1 tells us, "Among the prophets and teachers of the church at Antioch of Syria were Barnabas, Simeon (called "the black man"), Lucius (from Cyrene), Manaen (the childhood companion of King Herod Antipas), and Saul." (NLT)

The church in Antioch was exploding with growth—not only numerical growth, but also spiritual growth. Numerical growth is seen in Acts 11:21, "A great number believed and turned to the Lord." Then Acts 11:24 says, " . . . and a great many people were added to the Lord." Spiritual growth is seen in Acts 11:26 where we are told, "They assembled with the church and taught a great many people."

Barnabas and Paul allowed John Mark to see how ministry was being done in a rapidly growing, multiethnic, church-planting church. This ministry experience would have been a different experience than the one in the Jerusalem church. This experience would have pushed John Mark out of his comfort zone. This exposure allows us to see another aspect of John Mark's personality. He was willing to try new things.

Leaders, as we look for new leaders, let's be on the lookout for disciples who are willing to get out of their comfort zone. Even if they are taking smaller steps than you hope, it's still progress in the right direction. Yes, they will probably be nervous because they are trying new experiences; but if they are willing to try something new, begin to have some conversations about possible leadership opportunities. As we scan our ministries, we should keep our eyes open for people who are willing to go with us as we try new things. And remember, small progress is still progress.

I am of the opinion that leaders should be cautious around people who aren't willing to move out of their comfort zone and not willing to try something new. This shows they are not willing to grow, and this behavior will not only limit their future, but also the future possibilities of the church. I am not saying these individuals are bad people; I'm only pointing out that these individuals will put a lid on your expansion and innovation. Give me the person who is willing to try something new and willing to learn, over the person who is stuck in their ways and think they know it all.

BACK TO SIMPLE APPRENTICESHIP

Preparation:

Let's return to Jesus's simple model of apprenticeship that the Fergusons wrote about in *Exponential* and talk about preparation. John Mark's exposure to ministry in the early church would have been preparation for a life of leadership ministry in extremely diverse cities. John Mark was being exposed to what God was doing in his church as it was unfolding. He would have seen how two different churches (Jerusalem and Antioch) were sharing the Gospel and making disciples while learning from seasoned leaders. Apprenticeship should prepare disciples to do leadership ministry in a local church within the diverse cities of the world. I believe the best place to develop church leaders is in the local church.

While we have not completely perfected the preparation aspect of apprenticeship at Mt. Calvary, we do have a process in place to prepare disciples for leadership roles within the church. We want to prepare the emerging leaders God sends us while working with God as he moves them into leadership.

Here is an overview of the process:

First, the apprentice goes through the Leadership 501 Growth Track class. Currently, I teach this class which exposes apprentices to our expectations and prepares them for the apprenticeship process.

Next, we want them to attend a bi-monthly leadership training which we call the Leadership Gathering.

Third, we want apprentices to read books so they can learn our ministry and leadership philosophy. The two books we have them start with are:

- *Simple Church* by Thom Rainer and Eric Geiger, and
- *Develop the Leader Within* by John Maxwell.

Fourth, during their period of apprenticeship, we encourage apprentices to think about the ministry they want to lead. We want them to prayerfully consider what need God has placed on their heart to serve people. The apprenticeship process will eventually end, and apprentices need to be consulting God in prayer on their next steps as disciples and leaders with the church. This is a needed conversation because when the process is complete, that does not mean that apprentices will automatically take over the ministry where they did the apprenticeship. The current leader may still want to continue leading the ministry. The apprentice needs to seek God about what He wants them to do. Such as:

- Start a new ministry.
- Take over a ministry where a leader is needed.
- Continue to serve in the ministry and help the current leader.
- Join a new ministry and help the leader of that ministry.

This is a conversation that I usually have with apprentices doing the Leadership 501 class; but I have been encouraging our leaders to begin to have this conversation with their apprentices as well. That way, apprentices see that our leadership is invested in them following Jesus into the leadership role he has planned for them.

Finally, when it comes to our leaders training apprentices to do the tasks of the ministry and leadership, we use the simple process we learned from John Maxwell's book, *Developing the Leader Within You.*[19]

The process is as follows:

- Leader does. Apprentice watches. Discuss what happened.
- Leader does. Apprentice helps. Discuss what happened.
- Apprentice does. Leader helps. Discuss what happened.
- Apprentice does. Leader watches. Discuss what happened
- Apprentice becomes a leader. Find an apprentice.

The above process is best used initially with giving the apprentice a specific task. This gives him or her time to learn the ropes of the ministry. This allows the apprentice to shadow the leader while leading, so the apprentice can learn and grow. In this way, leadership is caught and taught. As the apprentice progresses, additional responsibilities may be given. This process can be used toward having the apprentice eventually run the ministry as a whole.

Where we have fallen short in our preparation of apprentices in the past few years is in performing scheduled feedback in the apprentices' progress—letting them know where they are in the process, and how they were performing and growing. We were not letting them know what they needed to work on and what they were doing well. As a result, people lingered too long in the process, they were unsure of their next steps, and became frustrated with the process. We have been working through our feedback process and encouraging our leaders to set up regular update sessions with their apprentices. We will discuss this further in chapter four.

SENT OUT

John Mark was at Antioch when God called Barnabas and Saul out on their first missionary journey to plant churches. The Bible tells us that when Barnabas and Saul left Antioch, they took John Mark with them and he was "their assistant" (Mark 13:5).

We don't know what the title involved. Neither do we know the ministry responsibilities, but we do know it was a promotion. He didn't have the title of assistant when they left Jerusalem, but now he does.

Graduation:

Looking at the final section of Jesus's simple apprenticeship process of graduation, we see that John Mark has graduated to another level in ministry. He has a title, and titles come with responsibilities. He is given more opportunity to do ministry with new responsibilities. Some would say when John Mark became their assistant, then he entered into the apprenticeship process. While that could be the case, it may also be seen as moving forward to a new position within the apprenticeship process.

The graduation portion of the apprenticeship process is important. I will be honest with you; this was not on my radar until I began working on clarifying our process. This is something new we have added to our apprenticeship process. I have been thinking about what graduation looks like at Mt. Calvary. I came up with multiple ideas; but for now, we are looking at a two-step process. First, when a disciple completes the requirements to become a leadership apprentice, the individual should be recognized. While it will not be a formal celebration, we will tell our leadership team that a new apprentice has been added, and the ministry where the apprentice is serving will be informed that he or she is an apprentice now.

Secondly, when the disciple completes the apprenticeship process, we will do some kind of formal recognition. We will mention during our worship service that the person has completed the apprenticeship process. We will also give a certificate of completion. As I reflected on graduation, it is an important part of the apprenticeship process which we have overlooked. The graduation helps the apprentice know there is something to look forward to. The apprentice must know he or she will not be an apprentice forever.

The graduation is also an indication that the apprentice is ready to take on more responsibility (work) within the church. As a side note, as leaders, we must be on the lookout for people who are willing to take on more responsibility whether they are in the apprentice process or not. As disciples mature in their faith, and are looking to take on more responsibilities, we should delegate it to them.

I'm not talking about people who are only looking for a title and a promotion. I'm speaking of people who are ready, willing, and able to take on more work. The work may come with a title, but the main thing is not the title, but, rather, the people who are willing to do the work that comes along with the title.

It's disheartening to encounter people who want titles without responsibility. It doesn't matter if we are talking about in the church or in the marketplace. Friend, who cares if you are a pastor if you aren't studying to preach and teach, guarding the flock, equipping the saints, and loving the church and your community? Who cares if you are a politician if you aren't serving and protecting your community and helping those people to prosper, grow, and be safe? The questions at the end of the day for leaders and apprentices are, "Are you doing the work that comes along with the title?" and "Are you willing to commit to doing the work before you have the title?"

ON THE MISSION FIELD

John Mark was with Barnabas and Paul at Paphos when God used Paul to blind the false prophet Bar-jesus, and lead the proconsul of Paphos, Sergius to salvation. Now that would have been an amazing mission trip be a part of. I can only image what John Mark thought when he saw the power of God blind a man and save another man in the same city. Then we are told when they leave Paphos and travel to Pamphilia, John Mark leaves them and returns to Jerusalem (Acts 13:13).

Luke does not tell us why he left, but we do know he left. When you read commentaries, people speculate why he left, but the truth of the matter is that we don't know. It could have been for any number of reasons.

F.F. Bruce writes, "Perhaps he did not care for the increasing rigors which evangelization of Asia Minor would involve; perhaps he resented the way in which his cousin Barnabas was falling into the second place. (When the expedition set out from Syria, the order is 'Barnabas and Saul'; by the time they leave Cyprus it is 'Paul and his company'!)"[20] Or it could have been something completely different. We are not told.

The same thing happens today. Many times we don't know why people leave our leadership teams, ministries, churches, or organizations. Most of the time there isn't an exit interview; and if there was, they probably wouldn't tell you everything. So really, we don't always know why people leave.

But whatever the case, we don't have the leisure to take it personally. People leaving is a part of the territory of leadership. Everyone will not stay with you as you lead, and that's okay. Our responsibility is not to keep people with us, but to help prepare them for what God wants to do with them.

When we take people leaving personally, it can send us into a downward spiral of negativity toward developing future leaders. We begin to ask questions like, "Who will leave?" or "When will they leave?" The next line of questioning moves to "Why should I invest in them if they are going to leave?" and "Why should I waste my time on someone who will not stay around to help me?"

When we think like this, we are trying to protect ourselves and our feelings. But this sequence of questions does not benefit anyone—not you (the leader), the future leader, nor the church. A better question for us to ask is, "Are we doing our part to develop new leaders while they are with us?"

If we truly care about making disciples and developing the next generation, we must teach them, even though some of them will leave us. We must train them, even though some of them will move on with our knowledge. We must mentor and develop them, even if they will exit our churches.

Leaders, we must remember people left Jesus, and he is the greatest leader there ever was. People stopped following him to walk with him no more. And we know he knew who would leave him, but he was still willing to teach, train, mentor, develop, and even die and resurrect for them.

Even as I am typing, I can hear some leaders saying, "Well, I'm not Jesus." No, but that's who God is trying to conform us into, the image of his dear Son (Rom. 8:29). A few of his molding tools are pain, rejection, and being forsaken by people. But it's not to break you, it's to make you into a leader that radiates the glory of Jesus.

As leaders, we too, must take heed to the wisdom of Ephesians 5:1 where it says, "Be imitators of God as dear children." We must keep our hearts tender toward God and his people so we can work with him to develop leaders within his church. Everyone who starts the process will not finish the process and that's okay. Leave that part to God. We just need to develop the disciples he sends our way.

EXERCISE:

1. What process do you have to locate potential leaders?

____

____

____

2. What is your apprenticeship process?

____

____

____

3. What expectation and goals do you have for your apprentices?

____

____

____

4. How will you work through people disappointing you and leaving the process or church?

____

____

____

NOTES:

CHAPTER 4: FACING FAILURE

"He needs development as a person even more than he needs development as a manager."

- Peter Drucker [1]

"Think of the worst thing you've ever done. Now what if that was the only thing you were known for?"[2] That is a rather sobering question to think about and answer. That question was asked by Andrew Glazier in a video in a Forbes.com article. Glazier is the CEO of Defy Ventures which is a prison entrepreneurial reentry program. He goes on to say in the video "That's the best way to think of the stigma that someone faces when they come out of prison."

The incarceration rate in America surpasses every other country in the world. "The U.S. has 5% of the world's population, but 25% of the world's prisoners."[3] For many in the prison system, recidivism is a real possibility, especially if they don't find employment. To help those who are incarcerated, or were previously incarcerated, with a real chance to employment and a changed life, Defy Ventures enters prison with hope. While the national recidivism rate is 30%, the rate for those who graduate from Defy is at 8%.

Defy Ventures, operating in 7 states and 18 prisons, offers a seven-month curriculum. They offer classes on character, personal development, parenting, and business coaching to those in prison. When someone completes the program, they experience a graduation and participate in a Shark Tank-style pitch contest on their new business proposal. With over 5,200 EITs (Entrepreneurs in Training) participating in the program, they have seen lives change.

A major catalyst for changing people's lives is *community*, which Defy Ventures emphasizes. Defy has a powerful force of 4,800 volunteers (CEOs, Managers, Entrepreneurs) who go into prisons as business coaches. They aren't there to give sympathy and a handout; they are there to encourage, challenge, and give a hand up to those who want to change. It is a daunting task to change when you're seen through the lens of your failure and no one is in your corner to cheer you on as you walk through your transformation.

No matter what phase of life you are in, you will experience failure. It may not be a failure like those whom Defy Ventures serve, but we all will experience it. Failure is a part of life and learning. But it doesn't have to define you. Rather, if we are continual learners, our failure can actually refine us.

Two areas leaders should help disciples, apprentices, and developing leaders work through are failure and disappointment; because, the truth of the matter is that we all will face those two things from time to time. As we help disciples move through the Next Leader Continuum, the center circle—facing failure and disappointment (emotions)—will be a recurring theme as we help people develop. And that's okay, especially if we are learning from them.

Next Leader Continuum

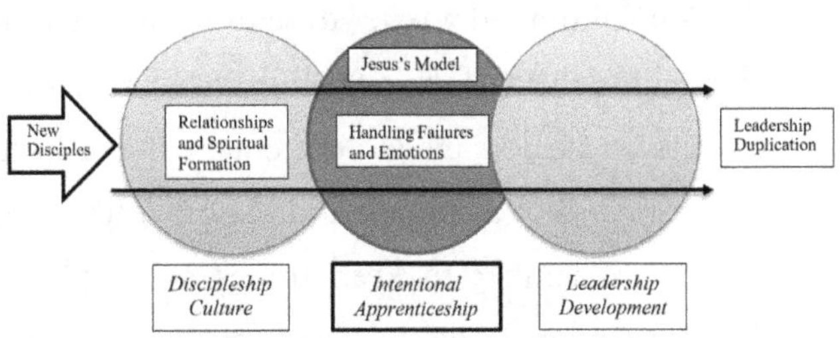

JERUSALEM COUNCIL

When we meet up with John Mark again, it's in Acts 15 after the Jerusalem Council. At this council, the first-century church leadership worked through the requirements of salvation for all people—Jews and Gentiles, which still applies today.

Verse 1 of Acts chapter 15 opens by giving us the reason why the council was initiated, "Certain men came down from Judea and taught the brethren (at Antioch) [that] 'Unless you are circumcised according to the custom of Moses, you cannot be saved.' " After a sharp dispute between the men at Antioch, and Paul and Barnabas, they all went to Jerusalem to sort out the requirements for salvation. The council declared in verse 11, "We believe that through the grace of the Lord Jesus Christ we shall be saved." Salvation does not come through anything we can do, it is given to us because of Jesus's death and resurrection.

The council drafted a letter to send to the Gentile churches telling them of their conclusion. In the letter, the apostles and elders made a statement that I have hanging in my office at church and at home. It's there to help me remember to keep things as simple as possible so we can make disciples and develop emerging leaders. The statement is from Acts 15, verse 28, "For it seemed good to the Holy Spirit and to us to lay upon you no greater burden than these essentials" (NASB). We want to make sure we are not complicating the process of making disciples or leaders.

The council commissioned Paul, Barnabas, Judas, and Silas to take the message to the churches. Then we find out as we continue reading chapter 15, that John Mark went with them. He travels with them all the way back to the church in Antioch. When Paul and Barnabas were ready to go on their second missionary journey to check on the churches they had planted, we are told that Barnabas wanted to take John Mark again, and Paul sharply disagreed, which caused Paul to part company from Barnabas and John Mark.

DO OVER

Before we deal with these two leaders, let's take a moment to look at John Mark. Let me point out that John Mark is willing to go back out with them, after he deserted them on the first journey. I believe this is a positive quality being shown in John Mark. He could have said, "No thank you. I was only planning to come to Antioch."

However, John Mark was willing to try the experience again, even though it did not work out well the first time. Dr. Warren Wiersbe mentions a statement author A. T. Robertson wrote about Mark, saying he had " 'flickered in the crisis, but the light did not completely go out.' This is an encouragement to all of us."[4]

Leaders, there is something very hopeful and encouraging going on in the heart of an aspiring leader who says, "Yeah, I messed up, but if you let me try again, I'll do it." Yes, they fell down and scraped their knees, but they are willing to get up and try again. And we should encourage them to try again.

As leaders, we should be looking for people who are "failing forward"—grabbing the title from one of John Maxwell's books. We cannot abandon people who have messed up on an assignment. Instead, we should be asking ourselves, Who's learning from their mistakes?

____

____

If people are learning from their mess-ups, they are growing. Learning from failure is a commendable quality. They are turning their losses into lessons. We must remember that aspiring leaders are not the only ones who fail. Seasoned leaders fail as well. Leaders should encourage themselves and their apprentices to "fail well" by learning from their failures.

LEARNING PROCESS

In *Practicing Greatness* by Reggie McNeal, in his chapter on the Discipline of Self-Development, he has a section on Developing Through Failure. He opens the section by writing, "Although no one wants to get really good at failure, leaders need to learn to deal with the inevitable." He goes on to say, "Some failures seek you out; others are self-manufactured. All failures present the leader with choices of how to deal with the failure. Whether to shrink or to grow. Whether to learn or derail."

Aren't those words true? As leaders and aspiring leaders, we will encounter failure but we will also realize we have the ability to choose how we will respond to it. McNeal lets us know the wrong thing to do when we fail is to go into "blaming, hiding, recriminating, excusing, diverting" because these "practices compound the failure."[5]

In this section, McNeal gives eight practices to use to help us develop through failure.[6]

1. Admit the Mistake.

   When we admit we have made a mistake, it shows we are people of character. He indicates that this display of character becomes more difficult the higher we go up the leadership ladder.

McNeal says, "The key is to be specific. What, exactly, was the mistake? Was it poor moral choices? Was it failure to pay attention to something? Whatever it was, name it."

2. Accept Responsibility.

When things go wrong, don't pass the buck. Do not blame someone else if you're the leader. The buck stops with you. McNeal mentions Jim Collins's observation about a Level 5 Leader:

They "use both windows and mirrors. When things are going well, they point out to all the people beyond them who make it possible. When things don't go well, these same leaders stand in front of the mirror and take responsibility for the failure."

3. Make Restitution.

McNeal writes, "Sometimes saying 'I'm sorry' is not enough." To prove his point, McNeal talks about Zacchaeus paying restitution to the people he extorted money from. For clarity's sake, McNeal writes, "His acts of restitution did not save him, but they proved the authenticity of his conversion experience and the seriousness of his new faith."

4. Reassess Life Vision and Values.

   Failure should cause a leader to look within and examine his or her life, motives, actions, and objectives. But we can't stop there. We must also examine our values. McNeal writes, "Often failed values account for the failure itself: integrity may have been compromised; relationships may have been damaged. The attention to values will bring the leader back to center."

5. Mourn Your Loss.

   As McNeal says, "Failure involves loss. The losses may include relationships, credibility, leadership influence, self-esteem, or sense of direction." Because this is the case, the experience of loss needs to be mourned if you are going to move forward from the failure.

   How you grieve, when you grieve, who you grieve in front of, and who you grieve with will require some wisdom because everyone will not appreciate your grief or help you through the grieving process.

6. Move to Closure.

   Even though you grieve, you can't linger in the state of grief. You have to experience the grief and then move on because things must get done and people are looking for you to lead. McNeal writes, "Followers need the confidence that the leader is on the job, not mired down by one episode of failure."

7. Accept Direction.

   McNeal informs us, "The level of guidance a leader needs depends on the failure." All failures are not equal. They don't all need the same level of intensity or formality. It all depends on the failure. The failure could be program related, personal, moral, poor decision making, etc. But whatever the case, we will need new information and direction to move forward. So, we will need to read, talk with mentors or wise friends to help us learn from our mistakes, and chart a new course.

8. Establish New Behaviors and Accountabilities.

   The old cliché is still true, to do the same thing over and over and expect a new result is insanity. Learning from our failures is shown by a change in our behaviors and by doing something different. This may include getting some accountability partners and putting new accountability measures in place so you can maintain the new behavior.

We must learn from our failures and encourage others to do the same. In John Mark's case, we don't know if it was an actual failure from something John Mark did wrong. And if it was a failure, we aren't told in the Scriptures if the failure was a sin, if he was being rebellious, or if he was being disobedient to God. The Bible doesn't specifically say why John Mark left them in Pamphylia.

Yet, even if the person who has failed finds their failure a result of rebellion or disobedience, we should not be quick to cut them off and dismiss God's plan for their life. If the person repents and shows fruits of repentance, and he or she walks through the steps of restoration, the Bible tells us, "ye who are spiritual, restore such an one in the spirit of meekness; considering thyself, lest thou also be tempted" (Galatians 6:1, KJV). We must be careful because we could be the next one to fall. The restoration may not be to the same position the individual held before the fall, but there should be definite restoration back to Christian fellowship.

PEOPLE PERSPECTIVE

Now, back to the dynamic duo, Paul and Barnabas. They split their ministry over a disagreement concerning John Mark. Acts 15:39–40 says, "Their disagreement was so sharp that they separated. Barnabas took John Mark with him and sailed for Cyprus. Paul chose Silas, and as he left, the believers entrusted him to the Lord's gracious care" (NLT). John Mark goes with Barnabas back to Barnabas's home city of Cyprus.

Using this experience with Paul and Barnabas, Dr. Warren Wiersbe writes in his commentary about the lens leaders look through when they think about people. He says that the way Paul saw people was through the question, "What can they do for God's work?" This speaks to the fact that people are tools in the hand of God. People are instruments of God to be used for the glory of God.

When he writes about Barnabas, he says the way he views people is through the question, "What can God's work do for them?" This lens sees people as God's masterpiece and handiwork—that God is using the assignment to make something out of the person he has called to the work.[7]

Both questions are important and both questions must be asked. But whichever lens you lean on the most, speaks volumes about you, your leadership style, and your view of people. In a perfect world this is a both/and conversation. We must see people through both lenses.

If I had to choose, I would choose the lens of Barnabas. For me, people aren't just tools. They are not a means to an end. They are God's handiwork and God is fashioning and transforming them as they obey him and do his will.

I am all for excellence, but I'm for salvation and sanctification more. I want to get things done and get positive results. I want to be effective (do the right things) and efficient (right way). But not more than I want people to get into the game, find their gifts, develop into leaders, and become mature disciples of Christ.

I ascribe to the ministry philosophy that Dave Browning speaks to in his book *Deliberate Simplicity* when he writes of the "80th percentile" rule of thumb. He writes, "In a Deliberately Simple church, we tend to use the 80th percentile as our rule of thumb. Will the new person be able to execute his or her role at least 80 percent as well as the person being replaced (or the person we would wish for)? If the answer is yes, we move forward, because we find that for most people, the difference between 80 percent and 100 percent, in terms of how it impacts their experience, is negligible."[8]

If those who you're looking for to serve and become apprentices can do 80% of the work, give them a chance. I will go as far as to say if they can do 70% of the work and they have a desire to learn and grow, then give them a chance. I know for the excellence-oriented (some would call perfectionist) folks, this sounds absurd. But what is more important, having perfectly executed stage lighting? Or helping a follower of Jesus on the path of being perfected in the image and stature of Christ? For me, it's the latter. This will require that the leader knows the most important tasks that have to be executed in the ministry.

I am of the opinion that Barnabas saw the potential in John Mark, and wanted to help cultivate it. I would also venture to say that Barnabas viewed John Mark's willingness to go out with them again, as John Mark's willingness to learn and grow from his previous experience.

After this moment in history, Barnabas and John Mark are no longer found in the pages of the book of Acts. Their names do not reappear until the prison epistles, specifically Philemon and Colossians.

MORE DEVELOPMENT

There are two other areas we must help emerging leaders work through. The first area is emotional growth and the other area is dealing with conflict. Both are areas where a leader will make mistakes and will need to grow. They are both areas that leaders will deal with on a continual basis.

I have had many personal sessions with the Lord working through emotional issues and seasons of conflict. I had to grow in both areas before I could help leaders grow emotionally and to courageously deal with conflict. Many issues leaders will face will cause them to confront their emotions. When there is a disagreement within the church, how a leader responds will speak volumes about his or her emotional maturity. The leader must also know how to confront the conflict in a Christ-honoring way.

We have already stated that in developing leaders, our main goal is not merely to develop church leaders, but to make disciples who are growing and maturing to become more like Jesus. Peter Scazzero made an interesting observation in his book *Emotionally Healthy Spirituality*. He wrote, "emotional health and spiritual maturity are inseparable. It is not possible to be spiritually mature while remaining emotionally immature."[9] He shows us how the fruit of the Spirit is not only about spiritual development, it is also about emotional growth. Scazzero shows the connection by lining up the fruit of the Spirit in both the *NIV Bible* and *The Message Bible*. Galatians 5:22-23:

NIV Bible	The Message Bible
Love	Affection for others
Joy	Exuberance about life
Peace	Serenity
Patience	A willingness to stick with things
Kindness	A sense of compassion in the heart
Goodness	A conviction that a basic holiness permeates things and people
Faithfulness	Involved in loyal commitments
Gentleness	Not needing to force our way in life
Self-Control	Able to marshal and direct our energies wisely

As you can see, *The Message Bible* translates the fruit in emotional language to help us connect them to everyday life. Not only must we make healthy progress spiritually, we must also make healthy progress emotionally. We must realize that God made every part of our being and that includes our emotions. Just like sin has affected us spiritually and physically, it has also affected our emotions. Many believers do not know how to express their emotions in healthy and godly ways. Therefore, our discipleship and leadership development must include growing healthy emotionally.

Scazzero also writes, "When we do not process before God the very feelings that make us human, such as fear or sadness or anger, we leak." He goes on to write, "Our churches are filled with 'leaking' Christians who have not treated their emotions as a discipleship issue. . . . Most people who fill churches are 'nice' and 'respectable.' Few explode in anger—at least in public. The majority, like me, stuff these 'difficult feelings,' trusting that God will honor our noble efforts. The result is that we leak through in soft ways such as passive-aggressive behavior (e.g., showing up late), sarcastic remarks, a nasty tone of voice, and giving the 'silent treatment.' "[10]

We must help people grow emotionally—because how disciples express their emotions, will affect how they love people. As the Great Commandment tells us, we are not only called to love God, we must also love people. And love is not just an internally-contained feeling. Love must be expressed in tangible ways toward people.

As Scazzero says, "Loving well is the goal of the Christian life."[11] We must "recognize that loving well is the essence of true spirituality. This requires that we experience connection with God, with ourselves, and with other people. God invites us to practice his presence in our daily lives. At the same time, he invites us 'to practice the presence of people,' within an awareness of his presence, in our daily relationships."[12] This is where we realize that not only are were growing in our relationship with God, we must also grow in our relationships with people.

Scazzero writes of four emotional stages that we are to help disciples grow through:

1. Emotional Infants
2. Emotional Children
3. Emotional Adolescents
4. Emotional Adults

We don't have time to dive into the components of the four stages, so I encourage you to check out Scazzero's books *Emotionally Healthy Spirituality* and *The Emotionally Healthy Church*. These stages are helpful reminders of where people may be emotionally in our church. Also, they help us begin to think through how we can help disciples grow emotionally and spiritually. People "need practical skills incorporated into their spiritual formation to grow out of emotional infancy into emotional adults."[13] The way we at Mt. Calvary are encouraging disciples and church leaders to grow emotionally is to encourage them to read Scazzero's book, *Emotionally Healthy Spirituality*.

One area our emotional stage is revealed is through conflict. Many believers handle conflict rather poorly and many do not know how to deal with it in a way that honors God. Scazzero gives two reasons why he believes disciples do not handle conflict well: "The first relates to wrong beliefs about peacemaking and the second relates to a lack of training and equipping in this area."[14]

When it comes to being a peacemaker, believers misinterpret Matthew 5:9 "Blessed are the peacemakers, for they will be called the sons of God." In this verse, God is not calling us to "be pacifiers and appeasers who ensure that nobody gets upset." Nor is he telling us to "ignore difficult issues and problems, making sure things remain stable and serene. When, out of fear, we avoid conflict and appease people, we are false peacemakers."[15]

Scazzero says, "The way of true peace will never come through pretending what is wrong is right! True peacemakers love God, others, and themselves enough to disrupt false peace. . . . Conflict and trouble were central to the mission of Jesus. . . . You can't have true peace of Christ's kingdom with lies and pretense."[16]

Scazzero also gives suggestions on how to be a good peacemaker. To get the full breakdown of his suggestion, please refer to his *Emotionally Healthy*

Spirituality book. Here are a few of his suggestions. They deal with speaking, listening, and respecting people.

- Speaking:[17]
  - Talk about your own thoughts, your own feelings (speak in the "I").
  - Continue speaking until you feel you've been understood.
  - When you don't have anything else to say, say, "That's all for now."
- Listening:[18]
  - Put your own agenda on hold. Be quiet and still as you would before God.
  - Allow the other person to speak until he or she completes a thought.
  - Reflect accurately the other person's words back to him or her. You have two options: paraphrase in a way the other person agrees is accurate or use his or her own words.
- Respecting people:

Scazzero reminds us that, "Respect is not a feeling. It is how we treat another person. Regardless of how we might feel about another human being, they are made in God's image and of infinite value and worth."[19] We must give people the space to be different, while at the same time take them seriously—as well as give people the benefit of the doubt because no one is perfect.

Another helpful resource that helps us deal with conflict is *The Case for Antioch*. In his book, Jeff Iorg has an entire chapter on conflict management. Iorg lets us know every church has conflicts and "church health isn't defined by the absence of conflict, but by how it's handled."[20]

Iorg tells us that the church in Antioch had to deal with its share of conflict: "It experienced disputes over doctrinal issues, tension with another church, discord among its leaders, and division over a personnel decision."[21] In his book, he shows how Antioch used five principles to work through its conflicts. Those principles are helpful for us to know:[22]

1. Anticipate conflict. Realize that conflict is going to happen in every church. Therefore,
    a. Study conflict management resources.
    b. Offer training on conflict resolution.
    c. Watch the horizon and minimize potential conflict situations before they explode.

2. Address conflict situations when they arise.
   a. You will have to confront the person(s) causing the conflict.
   b. This may mean having "one-on-one meetings, group meetings, and public comments as appropriate."[23]
   c. "Addressing the problem doesn't mean preaching a sermon to attack anyone, taking sides on an issue prematurely, or otherwise polarizing people needlessly. . . . Too often pastors preach a solution before they understand the issues at hand, firing nuclear salvos at BB-sized problems that could have been solved more effectively through a coffee shop conversation."[24]
3. Bring resolution to every conflict
   a. "To resolve, however, doesn't mean 'to solve.'. . . Conflicts in relationships don't often lend themselves to such precise endings. To resolve means to bring to the best conclusion possible, not end perfectly every time."[25]
   b. "The Bible . . . records two possible outcomes for conflict resolution among Christians: stay and work together or separate and work apart.

Ending kingdom-focused work wasn't an option. Sustaining conflict in a church wasn't an option. . . . Get together or move apart, but get on with kingdom work."[26]

4. Accept mixed results from conflict resolution.
    a. "Some conflict management involves compromise, particularly by leaders who may give up certain aspects of their agenda to get other items accomplished."[27]
    b. "Leaders who aren't willing to accept mixed outcomes in conflict resolution are doomed to perpetual frustration. . . . Wise leaders know when enough is enough and it's time to move on."[28]
5. Move on when resolution has been achieved.
    a. "Leaders must have the discipline to say, 'Enough,' and move their churches or organizations forward. . . . Being a leader also means you are wise enough to know when all that can be done has been done."[29]
    b. "To move on means agreeing on a resolution (even an imperfect one), putting the issue to rest, and shifting focus from the conflict back to accomplishing the mission of your church.

> Moving on is a disciplined choice to realign a church's focus, motoring toward the future rather than continuing to make pointless laps around the problems of the past."[30]

It's important to remember that conflict does not mean people are screaming and arguing. A conflict can be a difference in perspective that has to be worked through. But whether it is a difference of opinion, or an emotionally charged situation, we must help leaders learn how to handle conflicts courageously and compassionately. Conflicts must be addressed because we cannot let them stop us from making disciples and developing leaders. The mission is more important than our feelings, our fears, and our comfort.

EXERCISE:

1. What ways are you going to encourage apprentices to continue growing?

____

____

____

2. What failed experiences have you learned from that you feel comfortable sharing with emerging leaders?

____

____

____

3. How will you help disciples to grow emotionally?

____

____

____

4. What resources will you recommend for apprentices and leaders to learn how to deal with conflict?

____

____

____

NOTES:

CHAPTER 5: PERSISTENT PROGRESS

"It's not that I'm so smart,
it's just that I stay with problems longer."
Albert Einstein [1]

The year is 1974 and a gentleman by the name of Art Fry is singing in a West Virginia church choir. He is having a difficult time marking pages of his choir book for Sunday morning worship. In order to prepare for Sunday worship, he would tear off pieces of paper and place them in the book where the song was located. But he would find out, like most people who used torn off pieces of paper to keep their place in a book, one wrong move and the paper would fall out of the book losing his place. One day he thought to himself, "Gee, if I had a little adhesive on these bookmarks, that would be just the ticket."[2]

Fry had been to a seminar at his job a while back where one of his co-workers, Spenser Silver, had developed a lightweight adhesive, but the company did not have a viable market to distribute it at the time. Fry began experimenting with Silver's adhesive at work. His job had carved out time for their employees to pursue ideas and innovations. This time was known as the "15 percent rule." During his experimentation time, Fry applied the adhesive to little strips of paper and eventually came up with sticky temporary bookmarks. This idea of sticky temporary bookmarks weighed so heavy on Fry's mind as a potential commercial product, that he built a production machine to mass produce bookmarks in his basement.

Fry took the machine to his job and continued production of the sticky temporary bookmarks. The bookmark had a slow, difficult sales history at the beginning, but eventually it became one of the company's major product lines. When the product was first created, it was called Press and Peel tape. We would know the product today as Post-it® notes.

When I considered Fry and Silver's employer's "15 percent rule" of allowing their employees time to pursue their ideas on company time, it was revolutionary. So, I began to research the company they worked for and the name of the company is 3M (Minnesota Mining and Manufacturing Company). 3M did not start out as an organization that utilized the "15 percent rule." The rule was added to the company's culture and policy as 3M evolved. 3M realized they wanted their employees to have room to create products and be entrepreneurial within their organization.

When 3M began, it wasn't a profitable manufacturing company. It was a failed mining company. When the company was not able to locate a viable product out of the mine, it shifted courses. The company began using the grit from the mine to make sandpaper and grinding wheels. James C. Collins and Jerry I. Porras wrote in their book *Built to Last*, "from 1907 to 1914, the company struggled with quality problems, low margins, excess inventory, and cash flow crises."[3] Even though 3M had major issues at the beginning, the executives and employees refused to let the company die.

As 3M began to get its stability, the company encouraged employee initiative and innovation known as "experimental doodling."[4] The company realized their employees would make mistakes and every idea would not be profitable. 3M wanted to become a company that would evolve over time into a sustainable organization. In order to do that, they had to put processes in place that allowed them to take risks on the most valuable assets, their employees and their ideas. 3M did not only take ideas with the biggest market size from only its rising star employees. They were open to ideas from any employee in any market, no matter the size.

Collins and Porras write,

> Interestingly, however, 3M did not select innovations based strictly on market size. With mottoes like "Make a little, sell a little" and "Take small steps," 3M understood that big things often evolve from little things; but since you can't tell ahead of time which little things will turn into big things, you have to try lots of little things, keep the ones that work and discard the ones that don't. Operating "on a simple principle that no market, no end product is so small as to be scorned," 3M adopted a policy of allowing people to sprout tiny "twigs" in response to problems and ideas. Most twigs wouldn't grow into anything. But anytime a twig showed promise, 3M would allow it to grow into a full branch or perhaps even a full-fledged tree. This branching approach became so conscious at 3M that it sometimes explicitly depicted its product families in "branching tree" form.[5]

3M's consistent pursuit to evolve and become a better organization is inspiring. The desire to cultivate an environment where they don't give up on the organization and take risks on people, should encourage church leaders. If a group of executives can have that much passion in creating products and a company, our passion in the church must rise when it comes to making disciples and developing leaders so the church of Jesus can continue to expand. Even if we make mistakes along the way, we can never give up on people becoming disciples and future leaders. We must learn from our mistakes and continue to try to get better over time.

HE HAS GROWN

As we look into the life of John Mark, we find out that his leadership developed over time. And we must take that into account as we help disciples move into leadership roles within our churches. Leadership development isn't a one-time event; rather, it's an ongoing process.

When it comes to leadership development, Malphurs and Mancini have a good working definition. They wrote in *Building Leaders*, "Leadership development is the process of helping leaders at every level of ministry assess and develop their Christian character and to acquire, reinforce, and refine their ministry knowledge and skills."[6]

While our focus is on developing new leaders, we cannot forget about helping to develop current and seasoned leaders. Because, as Malphurs and Mancini remind us, "leadership development is never ending."[7] We can not only focus on developing apprentice leaders. We must also help current positional leaders become better as well.

From the time of Acts 15 and the Apostle Paul writing the prison epistles (Philippians, Ephesians, Colossians, and Philemon), at least 10 years have passed. In AD 60–61, the apostle Paul is in Rome under house arrest. This is his first imprisonment in Rome. It is during this time the Apostle Paul wrote the prison epistles.

In Paul's letter to his friend Philemon, he mentions John Mark as his "fellow laborer" (v. 24). That's interesting. John Mark isn't an assistant anymore. Nor is he a deserter. At the time of the letter, John Mark is the Apostle Paul's fellow laborer or co-worker. They are working together for Jesus.

Then in Colossian 4:10, Paul tells the church in Colossi that "Mark the cousin of Barnabas" is with him while he is in Rome. The Apostle Paul goes on to say in the verse, "if he comes to you welcome him."

We see some exceptional advisements in the life of John Mark. Not only is he Paul's fellow laborer, the apostle is recommending people to welcome John Mark and his leadership.

How did that happen? How has this young man changed so much over a decade? I would venture to say it was because God had placed some people in his life to disciple and mentor him. There were some people who allowed him to walk with them, even after he had messed up. There were people who saw his potential and refused to give up on him.

They took him through the Next Leader Continuum. (They didn't call it that. ☺)

1. Discipleship
2. Apprenticeship Process
3. Leadership Development

The next phase in the Next Leader Continuum is Leadership Development.

Next Leader Continuum

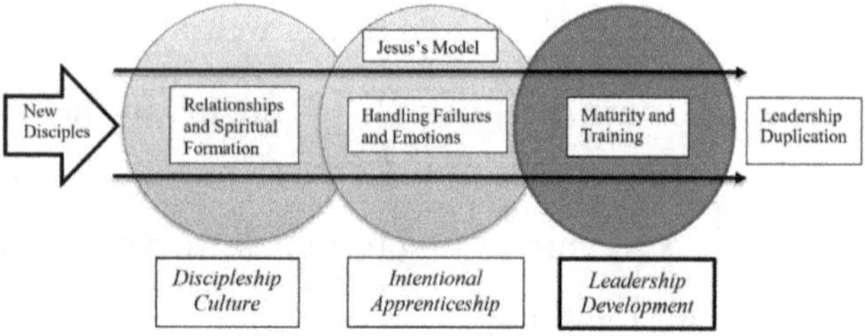

Jesus's Model

New Disciples

Relationships and Spiritual Formation

Handling Failures and Emotions

Maturity and Training

Leadership Duplication

Discipleship Culture

Intentional Apprenticeship

Leadership Development

We do not know what kind of training material they used, or what specific topics they wanted to make sure John Mark knew. But in our current ministry environments, future leaders need to be trained in areas such as:

1. Theology
2. Evangelism
3. Discipleship
4. Team Building
5. Vision Casting
6. Delegation
7. Outreach/Event Planning
8. Finances
9. Management
10. Systems/Process Development
11. Communication
12. Public Speaking

These topics are not in a specific order, but I do believe some should be taught sooner than others.

It is also helpful to have a process in place to help emerging leaders move through these topics and have a way to put them into practice. There are many ways churches are having people learn this information. Some require the emerging leaders to go to seminary. Others figure out what topics they want people to learn, then find books on the topics for the leaders to read. Others have created the material so it can be uniquely theirs and teach it to their leaders. Some are using pathways and curricula that their denomination created.

For example, the SEND Network created a process called Multiplication Pipeline to help develop future leaders from within the local church. It's a three-level learning platform available to all church members. It's a combination of online and book learning with assignments. The SEND Network also encourages the church to have a coach for those going through the Multiplication Pipeline.

The main thing is not what process and curriculum you are using to help develop your leaders, but rather, do you *have* a process that you're using to develop your leaders? You can always tweak the process later, but first you have to have a process to tweak. Leaders need to nail down a process so they can say, "This is how we develop leaders here." Whether you adopt a process or create one, you need a process for leadership development.

Church leaders need a systems approach to move people through leadership development. The track may split into different pathways depending on what kind of leader the disciple will be in the church. Some tracks have more curriculum and a longer development timeline and process. The more responsibility, influence, and visibility the disciple will have, the more training and development the leader will need. For example, for our ministers we will use the Multiplication Pipeline training created by SEND Network; but for our deacons we will use *The Deacon I Want to Be* training by Pastor Johnny Hunt.

A DECADE

I don't believe John Mark's development stopped with people being in his life. We have to include the 10-year time factor. During those 10 years, John Mark would have had multiple life experiences to help him grow up. Not only growing numerically, but also maturing spiritually, emotionally, mentally, and in capability.

While a 10-year time span and an increase in age doesn't automatically equate to more maturity, I believe in John Mark's case those things played a part in his life—especially based on the Apostle Paul's new response to him in Philemon and Colossians. After a decade, he who didn't initially seem to be a leader, has become a leader. Too often we overestimate how much people can mature in one year, and we underestimate the level of transformation that can occur over 10 years.

Leaders, it takes a long time to help develop emerging leaders. Then to add on to the length of time, leadership development takes a lot of work. Leaders, we must ask ourselves, "Are we willing to put in the work to develop future leaders?" I pray we are. As the famous coach Vince Lombardi said, "Leaders aren't born, they are made. And they are made just like anything else, through hard work."[8] Remember this when you get tired; it takes work to develop leaders.

Leaders, as you already know, God has a huge harvest awaiting us. And we need the local congregations and emerging leaders to help us reach our communities for Jesus. The words of Jesus are just as true as when he said them over two thousand years ago, "The harvest is great, but the workers are few. So, pray to the Lord who is in charge of the harvest; ask him to send more workers into his fields" (Matthew 9:37-38, NLT). The future workers are in our churches and are looking for us to help them develop into leaders who can reach the harvest. They are ready for us to mentor and develop them. But it will take time and hard work.

PETER'S TUTELAGE

Based on the timeline of the epistle, John Mark leaves the Apostle Paul and joins the Apostle Peter around AD 63. In 1 Peter 5:13, the Apostle Peter says, "Mark my son is with me and also is Silvanus in Babylon." Mark was Peter's spiritual son. Dr. Wiersbe writes, "It is a good possibility that John Mark was led to faith in Christ through the ministry of Peter."[9]

Historians aren't in agreement where Babylon was located. The *Life Application Bible Commentary* says, "Babylon has been broadly understood by believers to be a reference to Rome. . . . Most scholars suggest that Peter was in Rome when he wrote this letter and was sending greeting from the church there, the church being in Babylon and chosen together with the believers to whom Peter wrote."[10]

There are many Church fathers who affirm that Mark was with Peter in Rome and he wrote down the words of Apostle Peter.

Eusebius cites Papias, Bishop of Hierapolis in Asia Minor (AD 60–130), in his book *Ecclesiastical History*. He writes, "Peter makes mention of Mark in his first epistle which they say he wrote in Rome itself, as is indicated by him, when he calls the city, by a figure, Babylon." Papias also wrote, "The presbyter said, [elderly church leader, many believe it to be the Apostle John] Mark, having become the interpreter of Peter, wrote down accurately, though not indeed in order, whatsoever he remembered of the things done or said by Christ. . . . He followed Peter. . . . Mark committed no errors" in writing his Gospel.[11]

Then Justin Martyr, second-century Apologist in Rome (AD 100-165), said Mark had "written the memoirs of him" (Peter).[12]

Next, there is Irenaeus Bishop of Lyons, France (AD 180) who wrote, "Peter and Paul, however, were in Rome preaching the gospel and founding the church. After their departure, Mark, the disciple and interpreter of Peter, also delivered to us in writing the things that were then being preached by Peter."[13]

After that, there is Clement of Alexandria, the Bishop of Alexandria in Egypt in AD 195. He comments on 1 Peter 5:13 by writing, "Mark, Peter's follower [spectator] while Peter was preaching [praedicante] publicly the Gospel at Rome in the presence of certain of Caesar's equestrians [equitubus, i.e., members of the equestrian order] and was putting forward many testimonies concerning Christ, being requested [petitus] by them that they might be able to commit to memory the things that were spoken, wrote from the things that were spoken by Peter the Gospel that is called, 'According to Mark.' "[14]

Dr. Oden mentions how "Tertullian (ca.150–220) also argued that 'the Gospel which Mark published [edited] is affirmed to be Peter's, whose interpreter Mark was.' "[15]

Then we have Origen of Alexandria (AD 230) who comments on all four Gospels saying, "As I have understood from tradition, respecting the four gospels, which are the only undisputed ones in the whole church of God throughout the world. [*sic*] The first is written according to Matthew, the same that was once a publican, but afterwards an apostle of Jesus Christ, who having published it for the Jewish converts, wrote it in the Hebrew. The second is according to Mark, who composed it, as Peter explained to him, whom he also acknowledges as his son in his general Epistle, saying 'The elect church in Babylon, salutes you, as also Mark my son.' And the third, according to Luke, the gospel commended by Paul, which was written for the converts from the Gentiles, and last of all the gospel according to John."[16]

Lastly, there is Jerome (AD 340–420), "Mark, the interpreter of the Apostle Peter, and the first bishop of the church of Alexandria, who himself has not seen the Lord, the very Savior, is the second [who published a Gospel] but he narrated those things, which he had heard [his] master preaching, more in accordance with the trustworthiness of the things performed than [in accordance with their] sequence."[17]

ANOTHER ELEVATION

As we think about John Mark writing down the words of the Apostle Peter, we see again Mark is elevated. He has been given the grace to write down what the Apostle Peter had seen, heard, and experienced with Jesus. He became a scribe for the apostle to the Jews.

John Mark's Gospel arguably is seen as the first Gospel to be written. As mentioned back in chapter one, most scholars believe it to be the first Gospel account written, around early AD 50. Also, his account became something of a reference guide for Matthew (mid to late 50's) and Luke (late 50's, early 60's). The *Holman Study Bible* confirms this when it says, "Most Bible scholars are convinced that Mark was the earliest Gospel and served as one of the sources for Matthew and Luke."[18]

How did Mark get that opportunity? One, it was the grace of God. Secondly, he knew the Apostle Peter. There was an authentic relationship between them, where Peter called John Mark "son." He spent time with Peter listening, learning, helping, shadowing, and apprenticing. Finally, John Mark persevered through failure. He would not quit. He did not allow one moment in history to define him.

During John Mark's time with the leaders of the church, he would have seen the standard of leadership they lived by and the standard they wanted other church leaders to live by. When you read the prison epistles and 1st Peter, you can see how they spoke to the leaders within the churches on how to govern the congregations and how to live for Jesus.

As we think about developing leaders, I believe it's helpful to have a basic standard for all leaders within your church, regardless of their leadership position. It gives us a sense of consistency and accountability. At Mt. Calvary, we have 12 qualities of a leader and an Honor Code that leaders are to abide by. Our Honor Code is located in the Appendix. It's not original to us. We gleaned and honed from other churches.

Our 12 leadership qualities:

1. Leaders are disciples of Jesus. They love God and people.
2. Leaders live according to the Bible. They strive to live holy lives like Jesus.
3. Leaders are involved in and committed to Mt. Calvary's Discipleship Process and the Growth Track.
4. Leaders support and encourage other leaders within the church.
5. Leaders see the potential in people and want to see them grow into mature and committed followers of Jesus.
6. Leaders attend the Leadership Gatherings so they can be trained on how to be a leader.
7. Leaders lead ministry teams. He or she is the point person.
8. Leaders humbly lead by example first and by their words second.

9. Leaders make sure their ministries are operating effectively for the glory of God.
10. Leaders courageously confront problems within their ministry.
11. Leaders mentor (disciple) apprentice leaders within their ministry and encourage them to attend the Leadership Gathering. They are disciple makers.
12. Leaders train their ministry teams how to serve people with their gifts.

ENCOURAGE LEARNING

Before we close out this chapter, here are two suggestions to help leaders continue to grow: 1.) encourage self-development and 2.) practice evaluation through all levels of the church. Let's look at each one for a moment.

Encourage self-development:

Peter Drucker and Joseph A. Maciariello in their book entitled *Management*, write about the importance of self-development. They let us know that while companies and superiors have an important part to play in developing managers or leaders, "manager development is the responsibility of the individual."[19]

We must encourage apprentices and leaders to take ownership of their own development.

As Druker and Maciariello wrote, "Development is always self-development." Current leaders must model for others the importance of taking responsibility of their own personal, spiritual, and leadership growth—helping to understand no one can motivate them or make them develop. As leaders, we need to echo the sentiment of *Management,* "No one can motivate a person toward self-development."[20] . . . "The responsibility rests with the individual, her abilities, her efforts."[21] Whether we are sending apprentices and leaders through a pathway or process, or to a conference or workshop, they must take the material and develop themselves.

Druker and Maciariello also let us know, "The most important factors in self-development, apart from insights into one's own strengths, are experiences on the job and the example of the superior."[22] We have to let apprentices and leaders know that leaders are life-long learners. When leaders stop learning, they will eventually stop leading. Encourage apprentices and leaders to read books on Scripture, management, discipleship, volunteer ministry, church growth, emotional health, leadership, outreach, evangelism, personal growth, time management, and anything else that's not contrary to the Bible. A good idea would be to have a recommended reading list. Also, encourage them to read up on best practices of their ministry area so they can learn from other leaders and ministries.

Practice evaluation:

Another way to practice self-development is through self-evaluation, appraisals, and assessments—helping leaders look at their strengths and weaknesses. As mentioned in chapter two, we did not do well in this area, but we are working to turn that around by learning from those who do it well. One place we have learned this is from the book *Building Leaders,* by Malphus and Mancini.

In *Building Leaders*, Malphus and Mancini talk about the importance of evaluation and how evaluation should be done in all levels of leadership within the church. They mention four evaluations. They also give questions that are helpful during each evaluation. [23]

The first type of evaluation is the self-evaluation. The self-evaluation is for everyone in the organization—the leaders and the apprentices. The major question the leader is to evaluate himself/herself by is: How many leaders did I equip this past year? The apprentices have three questions: What have I learned? Where do I see growth? Where do I need improvement? The leaders can also use these three questions to help themselves grow.

Next, there are informal evaluations. These are ongoing evaluations. They are done as the leader observes the apprentice working and serving. On the spot, the leader lets the person know he or she is doing a good job or how to improve. A good book to help with this is *The One Minute Manager* by Ken Blanchard.

The third type of evaluation is the formal evaluation. This is done periodically—usually annually or every six months. The formal evaluation is generally a written document answering standard questions such as: What is this person doing well? In what areas does this person need to improve? What would you suggest that he or she do to improve? At Mt. Calvary, we have added questions such as: Who's your one? Who is your apprentice?

The final evaluation has to do with your leadership development process. When it comes to leaders, the question you want to ask is: Is the process actually developing leaders? Then when it comes to your apprentices, there are three questions you want answered: What did you like about the development process? What didn't you like about it? How could we do it better? While examining your process you want to evaluate curriculum, technology, and trainings.

Malphus and Mancini tell us, "The key to the evaluation is to focus on what your emerging leaders are doing well. . . . If leaders improve their weaknesses, at best they move from weak to average in those areas. . . . If they improve their strengths, however, they become even stronger and enjoy what they're doing in the process. Thus, you would be wise to harp on their strengths. . . . Remind them of and celebrate those strengths, point out newly discovered ones, and encourage them to continue to grow in them."[23]

I have learned in doing formal evaluations that a helpful technique is "the sandwich technique." Begin talking about their strengths and observed improvements. Then move on to their weakness and growth opportunities, and share how they can improve. Finally, move back to their strengths that should be developed, and close out the evaluation. This technique can also be taught to the other leaders so the technique can become a part of the culture of your church. That way, the church's leadership team is concentrating more on developing strengths instead of harping on weaknesses.

EXERCISE:

1. What leadership development process and material will you use?

____

____

____

2. What are your church's leadership qualities?

____

____

____

3. How will you help your leaders learn the importance of self-development?

____

____

____

4. What evolution process does your church have in place for your leadership?

____

____

____

NOTES:

CHAPTER 6: LEGACY BUILDING

"The Church needs leaders who build a culture of leadership development from a foundation of precise theological convictions."

Designed to Lead [1]

It's Sunday morning at 5am in Philadelphia, PA and St. George Methodist Church is having a worship service for its black members. The preacher who will be delivering the sermon is Richard Allen.[2] Rev. Allen has moved to Philadelphia after purchasing his freedom from his slaveowner, Stokely Sturgis, for $2,000.00 a few years earlier in 1783.[3] Richard Allen had been a traveling preacher for the Methodist Church since 1781.[4] He traveled "throughout South Carolina, New York, Maryland, Delaware, and Pennsylvania, preaching to black and white congregants alike."[5]

Allen became an assistant minister at St. George's leading prayer meetings for the black members.

Allen was a hard worker. Under his leadership, the prayer meetings grew. He would also go out to the black communities and preach. When he went out, he would sometimes preach four to five times a day. By the grace of God and his diligence, "he raised a society of 42 members, while he supported himself as a shoemaker."[6] But as the black membership grew at St. George's, so did the racial tension.

Initially, Allen had proposed that a separate building be built for the black members, which was rejected. The incident that caused the exodus of the black congregants from St. George's occurred in 1787. Some say it was around 1792–93 at a worship service.[7] Allen and another black minister, Absalom Jones, were kneeling to pray and one of the white church trustees told Jones they could not pray in that location. The trustee tried to force Jones to move, but Jones told him, "Wait until prayer is over, and I will get up and trouble you no more."[8] When prayer was over, all of the black congregants got up and left.

Allen and Jones left St. George's and founded the Free African Society to give aid to the black community. Out of that society, Richard Allen planted Bethel Church in 1794. Allen had to sue the Methodist church in Philadelphia because they attempted to control the congregation and Bethel's property. The suit went all the way to the Pennsylvania Supreme Court and on January 1, 1816, the court ruled in Allen's favor.

In April of the same year, Allen and several other black Methodist churches united to start the African Methodist Episcopal Church (AME) and Richard Allen was consecrated bishop of the newly formed denomination. The AME Church is the first black denomination in America. Not only did the AME Church grow, so did Bishop Allen's church. He pastored a mega church in the 1820s. His church had a membership of 7,500 members.

While Allen was an amazing church leader, he never stopped being a community leader. He fought against the atrocities of slavery. In 1830, he formed "the Free Produce Society, where members would only purchase products from non-slave labor."[9] Also, Bethel Church was one of the stops on the Underground Railroad. Runaway slaves would hide in the church's basement. Today the AME Church has over 6,000 local congregations and over 2.5 million congregants spread across "thirty-nine countries on five continents."[10] Allen's legacy is still inspiring people and Christians to this day.

As we come to the final chapter, I would like to remind us of the purpose of developing leaders in the church. The purpose of developing leaders is so we can make more disciples of Jesus. The focus is not to develop leaders for the sake of having more leaders. We develop leaders so more people can meet Jesus (salvation) and become like Jesus (sanctification).

MARK'S USEFULNESS

After John Mark was mentioned by the Apostle Peter, we find his name appearing again in the Scriptures. The final time he is mentioned is by the Apostle Paul again. Paul is in a dungeon in Rome, his second time being imprisoned in that city, and he is writing his last letter to Timothy around AD 66.

Paul says in 2 Timothy 4:11 to his protégé Timothy, that when he comes to see him to make sure he brings John Mark with him, "because he [John Mark] is useful to him for ministry." The *Life Application Bible Commentary* says, "We cannot be sure if Paul felt that Mark would be helpful to him personally, or if *helpful to me* refers to directing and facilitating the ministry outreach to the world. It's likely that both kinds of help were needed from Mark."[11]

How did Mark become useful? It wasn't through Paul's mentorship. It was through Barnabas's and

Peter's. They helped to develop him into the next leader in the church. But this we can celebrate concerning Paul: he did eventually forgive the failure of John Mark and he welcomed him into ministry with him (Philemon and Colossians).

Leaders who are willing to forgive and welcome people back into fellowship should be celebrated. Even though we are commanded to forgive, it isn't easy. From this vantage point, we see that the Apostle Paul has grown spiritually as well. From Paul's writings, we can observe that Paul realized he was still in the sanctification process (Philippians 4).

When we look through history, we find out not only does Mark write the Gospel of Mark, John Mark is also known by Christian tradition in Africa as being the "first apostolic missionary" to the continent of Africa, specifically to Alexandria in Egypt.

FIRST APOSTOLIC MISSIONARY

Dr. Oden writes, "In African narrative, Mark is remembered as having first planted the apostolic seeds of Christianity among his countrymen, the faithful Jews of Libya (Sawirus, HP, 141–42; Martyrium Marci 1). To say 'first' does not need to preempt the well-known testimony that even before Mark's missionary journeys, there were those at Pentecost speaking in

Libyan and Nilotic languages (Acts 2:10)." He goes on to say, "If the original participants at Pentecost other than Mark were the first to bring the good news to Africa, it still could be held that Mark was the first apostolically sent missionary to Africa."[12]

As Dr. Oden concludes, calling John Mark the "first apostolic missionary" is not to say that he was the first Christian or the first one to make disciples on the continent. We can look at other Scriptures to prove that point as well.

As mentioned above, there is Acts 2:10. That on the day of Pentecost there were Jews from Egypt, Libya (includes city of Alexandria), and Cyrene in Jerusalem, we can assume some of those individuals got saved and went back to their cities. All three of those cities are on the northern part of Africa.

Next, there is Acts 8:26–40, where we find out that Deacon Philip leads the Ethiopian eunuch to Christ on the southern outskirts of Jerusalem. We can assume from Scripture that the eunuch went back to Ethiopia, Africa, because he was a part of the royal court of Candance. Therefore, he would have taken his new faith with him.

Then in Acts 18:24–28, we are told about a Jewish man named Apollos who came from Alexandria, and he was a follower of Christ. While he may have needed to be taught more about Christ and the faith by Aquila and Priscilla, when he arrived in Ephesus "he spoke and taught accurately the things of the Lord" (Acts 18:25). Apollos was more than likely taught about Jesus in Alexandria, his hometown.

While there are some who will attempt to argue against John Mark being in Alexandria, Dr. Oden pushed against the idea that John Mark could not have been in Alexandria. He uses the tradition of Peter to prove his point.

Dr. Oden writes, "The hard physical evidence of Peter in Rome is no more compelling than of Mark in Alexandria. Both hinge on epigraphic residues and martyr memorials as well as literary recollections. Both arguments are based on large accumulations of circumstantial evidence. Why then is the authenticity of Peter's story so often assumed and Mark's so often denied? My hunch is that it is a Eurocentric predisposition that wishes to be regarded as valid scientific evidence."[13]

Bishop Eusebius cites the writings of Bishop Dionysius of Corinth on how Peter was in Corinth and Rome even though the Scripture does not specifically say he was there. He documents, "You have therefore by your urgent exhortation bound close together the sowing of Peter and Paul at Rome and Corinth. For both planted the seed of the Gospel also in Corinth, and together instructed us, just as they likewise taught in the same place in Italy and at the same time suffered martyrdom" (Eusebius CH 2.25).[14]

Then Dr. Oden writes about other well-known church leaders that declared John Mark was in Africa. He writes, "Many significant voices in primitive ecumenical Christianity have attested to Mark being in Africa—'the ancient presbyters' recalled by Clement, Eusebius, Jerome, and John Chrysostom."[15]

The same person who cited Bishop Dionysius concerning the Apostle Peter being in Rome also cites Clement of Alexander (AD 150–215). Bishop Eusebius writes, "They say that this Mark was the first that was sent to Egypt, and that he proclaimed the Gospel which he had written, and first established churches in Alexandria."

Then we have the fourth-century father Jerome (AD 340-420), writing about John Mark being "the first bishop of the church of Alexandria."

Finally, Dr. Oden shares, "John Chrysostom argued that Mark wrote or revised his Gospel in Egypt (Hom. Matthew 1)."[16]

This information is important because the church in Alexandria attributes its apostolic teaching and connection to the ministry of John Mark, which will be discussed shortly.

ALEXANDRIA

Alexandria was an amazing city. Nick Needham gives us a great description of the city of Alexandria in the first volume of his book *2000 Years of Christ's Power.* He writes,

> The Egyptian city of Alexandria was, after Rome, the greatest city in the Roman Empire. If Rome was the Empire's legal and administrative capital, Alexandria acted as its intellectual and cultural capital, as well as being one of its most important trading ports. It was the liveliest centre of artistic, scientific, and philosophical activity in the Greek and Roman world. A deeply Hellenistic community, it also had a vast Jewish population. Religious movements and ideas of every variety met and circulated in Alexandria, influenced each other, and were influenced by Greek philosophy.[17]

This reminds me of Barnabas and Paul taking John Mark to another influential city, Antioch. It, too, was an amazing, urbanized city with diversity and wealth.

We find out from the *African Memory of Mark* book by Thomas C. Oden, that John Mark made disciples in Alexandria.

Thomas Oden writes about Mark's first disciple in Alexandria, Anainus. Oden tells us where he obtained his information: "We are working from three analogous narratives, one early, one continuing in many editions, and one late—namely, (1) the pre-Eusebian *Martyrium Marci*, which is the basic pattern for Sawirus, (2) the synaxary versions that continue over the centuries but which lack early extant versions, and (3) the late first millennium, longer narrative of Sawirus."[18]

Martyrium Marci is The Martyrdom of Mark (sometimes call the Acts of Mark or History of Mark).[19]

"Martyrium Marci became one among many sources for Sawirus, who wrote the definitive history of the Coptic Patriarchs near the end of the first millennium."[20]

Sawirus [Sawirus (Severus), son of al-Muquaffa (Bishop) of al-Ashmunein] is a scholar and the bishop of al-Ashmunein. Al-Ashmunein is "the ancient Hermopolis Magna in the district of Antinopolis, near modern, Asyut." He was "one of our most important sources for the Coptic memory of Mark. . . . Sawirus was writing from about A.D. 955 to about 987."[21]

Synaxary is "an account of a martyr or saint—to be read at an early morning service—or a compilation of such accounts organized according to days of recollection of the Christian year in the ancient African church tradition."[22]

I will share an abbreviated version here, but for more details refer to Oden's book.

MARK'S FIRST DISCIPLE

We are told that John Mark met Anianus right after he entered the gate of Alexandria. A strap of Mark's shoe broke and he went over to a cobbler to fix his shoe. The cobbler was Anianus. In the midst of fixing Mark's shoe, Anianus cut his hand and screamed "God is One." The story goes on to say when Mark heard Anianus's words, he took that as confirmation that he was in the place God wanted him to be. Then Mark healed Anianus's wound.

Then Mark talks with him about his belief in God because he saw that Anianus was surrounded by "Greco-Roman and Egyptian deities" and Mark asked him, "If thou knowest that God is one, why dost thou serve these many gods?" Anianus replied, "We mention God with our mouths, but that is all; for we know not who he is" (Sawirus, HP, 143).[23]

After this exchange, Anianus asked Mark to come to his home to eat. "After they had eaten, the cobbler said to him: 'O my father, I beg thee to make known to me who thou art who hast worked this great miracle.' Then the saint answered him: 'I serve Jesus Christ, the son of the ever living God' (Sawirus, HP, 143).[24] The cobbler exclaimed: 'I would that I could see him.' The holy Mark said to him: 'I will cause thee to behold him' " (Sawirus, HP, 143).[25]

Oden goes on to write: "At this point the narrative of Sawirus moves from preaching the kerygma [gospel] to teaching its truthfulness. This points to the beginnings of catechetics as early as Mark's first Alexandrian conversation:

"Then he began to *teach* him the gospel of good tidings, and the *doctrine* of the glory and power and dominion which belongs to God from the beginning, and exhorted him with many exhortations and instructions, of which his history bears witness" (Sawirus, HP, 143–44, emphasis added).[26]

"[He] ended by saying to him: 'The Lord Christ in the last times became incarnate of the Virgin Mary, and came into the world, and saved us from our sins.' And he explained to him what the prophets prophesied of him, passage by passage" (Sawirus, HP, 144).[27] Then when the cobbler had heard wisdom and the words of the Scriptures from the holy Mark, together with the great miracle which he had seen him work upon his hand, his heart inclined toward him, and he believed in the Lord, and was baptized, he and all the people of his house, and all his neighbors. And his name was Annianus [Anianus]" (Sawirus, HP, 144).[28]

As we see here, Mark is making disciples of Jesus. He wanted to help people encounter the Risen Savior by proclaiming the name of Jesus.

EVERYONE MAKES DISCIPLES

Leaders, we must do the same thing today. We must be disciple makers. We must share the Gospel of Jesus Christ with the people we know and meet. But this is not only the responsibility of church leadership. Every disciple of Jesus is charged with the responsibility of making disciples of Jesus.

Because we desire that everyone (disciples and leaders) at our church, Mt. Calvary, obey Jesus's command to make disciples, we have inducted into the culture of our church the "Who's your one?" campaign (created by NAMB). Every disciple is encouraged to find one person he or she can pray for, care about, and share the Gospel of Jesus with. One person can't disciple the world, but everyone can be a disciple maker by telling one person about Jesus and encouraging that person to grow in their faith.

Because sharing the Gospel of Jesus is so important, we are equipping believers with methods for sharing the Gospel. There are many methods available today to share the Gospel effectively. But it does not really matter what method you use or teach your disciples to use. The main thing is that you and your church pick one or two and stick with them and teach them throughout the church. Then do refresher trainings on a regular basis to help the church practice sharing the Gospel. One helpful example I heard from a pastor on how his church does refresher trainings is whenever their church is about to do any kind of community outreach or connecting with the community, they do a training on how to share the Gospel.

Here are three methods with video resources on how to share the Gospel:

- 3 Circles (https://vimeo.com/227782208)
- Romans Road (https://www.youtube.com/watch?v=K9wSOwMYAhA)
- Four spiritual laws (https://www.youtube.com/watch?v=A_t1SJKMypU)

Which method will your church use?

____

____

Mark not only preached for people to be saved, he wanted to make sure they learned how to live for Jesus. He wanted them to learn the faith and the Word of God. His preaching moved into teaching.

ENCOURAGE QUIET TIME

When it comes to helping disciples learn the faith, one of the best practices we can encourage new believers to do is to begin to read the Bible daily. Encouraging them to begin a Bible reading plan is a good first step that can help them learn more about Jesus and how to be his follower. There are many ways this can be done, but here are a couple of suggestions to get started.

One way is to encourage the new believer to begin reading books of the Bible. A chapter a day or 15 minutes, to get them in the habit of reading the Scriptures. What I have been doing during my pastorate is encouraging people to read the Gospel of John, then the Gospel of Mark, and after that move on to the Book of Acts, and Romans.

Another way to encourage Bible reading is by having a corporate Bible reading plan—such as the whole congregation reading the New Testament in a year. When the person becomes a disciple, you can encourage him or her to join the church in reading the Scriptures. This corporate activity allows the church to move as a group through the Scriptures which encourages greater unity among the believers.

To help people get more out of their time of reading the Scriptures, we also encourage them to add journaling to their devotion time. We encourage believers to use a journaling method developed by Pastor Wayne Corderio (New Hope International) called S.O.A.P. SOAP is an acronym that stands for Scripture, Observation, Application, and Prayer. Pastor Corderio has a tutorial on Youtube.com that explains more of the process. (https://www.youtube.com/watch?v=Qo-Q8fUAA3k&feature=emb_title). The journal individuals use doesn't have to be fancy, unless they want it to be. But we encourage them to begin with an inexpensive wire-bound notebook that they can get from any store.

ONE-ON-ONE

As I thought about Mark's disciple-making process, it encouraged me to figure out a way to encourage our church members to find ways to move from preaching (sharing the Gospel) to teaching (discipling others). I was not sure how to get the concept of everyone being able to teach someone, into our church. Then in 2019, I went to a disciple-making seminar at Grace Church in Mentor, OH. While the weeklong seminar taught many things about creating a disciple-making culture in the local church, the component that shined through for me was how Grace Church infused one-on-one, inductive Bible studies into their church's culture. After the seminar I began to study their process.

After studying their process and reading *The Trellis and The Vine* by Colin Marshall and Tony Payne, the thought came to me to take the "Who's your one?" campaign a step further by adding a one-on-one disciple-making process. So, we are asking everyone to do an inductive Bible study with someone who is interested in knowing Jesus or growing to become like Jesus. This could be the same person they are praying for, caring for, and sharing Jesus with, or someone else. I'm not looking for us to add another program to our list of programs. My prayer is that this will become a part of who we are as disciple makers at Mt. Calvary.

I realize the one-on-one Bible studies is a slow process to get started within the church and to see the fruit that comes from its operation. But the beauty of this type of disciple making is that it can be done by Christians not looking to become leaders in the church. Therefore, they, too, will be growing in their walk with the Lord and focusing on making disciples of the Lord. We have included these one-on-one Bible studies into our small-group ministry format (See p. 50). Therefore, if individuals aren't in a small-group Bible study, they can use the one-on-one inductive Bible studies as their small group.

To help infuse one-on-one discipleship into the church's culture, it's helpful to use a simple curriculum. Some good resources are:

- *Church Growth International*—Charles Brook
    - o *Good News for You*
    - o *I Have Been Born Again, What Next?*
- *Grace Discipleship Series*—Grace Church of Mentor in Ohio
    - o *Foundations—Bible Truths for Christian Growth*
    - o *The Walk—Every Day Spiritual Growth*

The Trellis and the Vine book also has recommendations for a curriculum.

These one-on-one inductive Bible studies, along with your discipleship process, helps to create a catechism program (religious teaching and training) in your church. Not only will disciples grow in their knowledge of the Lord Jesus, but they will also be sharing the Gospel and discipling others. We will also see disciples practicing the "one anothers" of Scripture. Such as:

- Love one another (John 13:34. This command occurs at least 16 times)
- Build up one another (Romans 14:19; 1 Thessalonians 5:11)
- Accept one another (Romans 15:7)
- Admonish one another (Romans 15:14; Colossians 3:16)
- Care for one another (1 Corinthians 12:25)
- Serve one another (Galatians 5:13)
- Speak the truth in love (Ephesians 4:15, 25)
- Look to the interests of one another (Philippians 2:4)
- Teach one another (Colossians 3:16)
- Encourage one another (1 Thessalonians 5:11)
- Exhort one another (Hebrews 3:13)

- Stir up [provoke, stimulate] one another to love and good works (Hebrews 10:24)
- Show hospitality to one another (1 Peter 4:9)
- Employ the gifts that God has given us for the benefit of one another (1 Peter 4:10)
- Pray for one another (James 5:16)

Including these three components into our church at Mt. Calvary will help us push the roots of discipleship deep into our culture. We are encouraging disciples to make disciples. That requires us to teach people how to share the Gospel, how to spend quality quiet time with God, and how to practice the "one anothers" through one-on-one Bible studies. This process will not be easy or quick, yet it will be worth it to see disciples of Jesus maturing in their walk with Christ.

SCHOOL OF ALEXANDRIA

It is said that it was John Mark's teaching that sparked the eventual creation of one of the greatest catechetical programs in history, the School of Alexandria. As Dr. Oden writes, "Mark was from the outset a catechist. . . . Preaching and teaching were his central purposes."[29] It is also said that John Mark's catechism and pattern of exegesis was the seedbed for the School of Alexandria.

This School of Alexandria "was the hub of Christian intellectual and literary development and Christian preaching that was grounded in the Hebrew Scriptures. Coptic sources hold that it was Mark who started a catechetical system for the edification of the newly converted catechumens."[30] While John Mark didn't start the school, his influence, teaching, and preaching helped to lay the school's foundation.

Some scholars attempt to downplay the role of the Alexandrian School in history. But, "The Alexandrian School is the first of its kind and a model for all subsequent expressions of Christian higher education. . . . Its patterns of exegesis were soon followed in Carthage (Tertullian), Caesarea (Origen), Cappadocia (Gregory of Nazianzus), and Rome (Gregory the Great)."[31]

Some scholars also attempt to tarnish its reputation by saying the Alexandrian school was a place of mysticism. Dr. Oden points out, "The school was known more for unchanging transmission of the apostolic faith than for presumptuous forms of originality or individual creativity."

He goes on to write, "Origen, who headed the Catechetical School, is sometimes portrayed as the most original of the early African writers. But it was he who insisted that 'the teaching of the church is preserved unaltered handed down in unbroken succession from the apostles and existing to this day in the churches' " (First Principles Pref. 2).[32]

LAYERING

A catechism program can be seen as adding another layer onto your discipleship process. This is where you can help disciples who aren't leaders, grow toward maturity. Leaders are not the only people required to grow; all disciples must grow.

Jeff Iorg says something interesting in *The Case for Antioch* about "layering" our disciple making. He writes, "Transformational churches use a 'layered' approach rather than a sequential approach to making disciples. A layered approach means the church uses multiple methods at the same time to train disciples. This means some members will be in one-on-one relationships, others in closed groups, others in open groups, while still others only in large groups."

He goes on to say, "Some will participate in multiple opportunities at various levels at the same time. Others will participate in more than one level but on a pick-and-choose basis. Rather than a 'you all come' approach that seeks to involve every member in every learning activity, a healthy church creates a menu and challenges people to engage the process at the appropriate level."[33]

Another helpful resource and perspective when it comes to helping disciples grow through a catechetical program is the book *Real-Life Discipleship* by Jim Putman. In the book, Putman describes the discipleship process his church uses to make disciples and to help them grow toward maturity.

Real Life Ministries, the church Putman pastors, uses a five-stage process for making disciples and spiritual growth:[34]

- *Spiritually dead:* They are characterized by unbelief.
- *Spiritual infant:* They are characterized by ignorance.
- *Spiritual child:* They are characterized by self-centeredness.
- *Spiritual young adult:* They are characterized by service, God-centered and other-centered.
- *Spiritual parents:* They are characterized by Intentionality, Reproducibility and Strategy.

In *Real-Life Discipleship*, Putman gives recommendations on books his church suggests to individuals based on their current stage of discipleship to help them grow spiritually.

At Mt. Calvary, when disciples ask what books they can read, individually or in one-on-one Bible studies, to help with their spiritual development we recommend:

- Reading the Gospel of John
- Bible reading plan
- *20 Christian Beliefs Every Christian Should Know* by Wayne Grudem
- *Experiencing God* by Henry T. Blackaby and Claude V. King
- *Emotionally Healthy Spirituality* by Peter Scazzero
- *Financial Peace* by Dave Ramsey
- *Developing the Leader Within* by John Maxwell
- *The Kingdom Agenda* by Tony Evans
- *Theology You Can Count On* by Tony Evans

LEADERSHIP DUPLICATION

As we will see in a moment, John Mark moves into a new phase of his ministry where he is developing new church leaders within the church in Alexandria.

The purpose of duplicating leaders is so the church makes more disciples of Jesus.

Next Leader Continuum

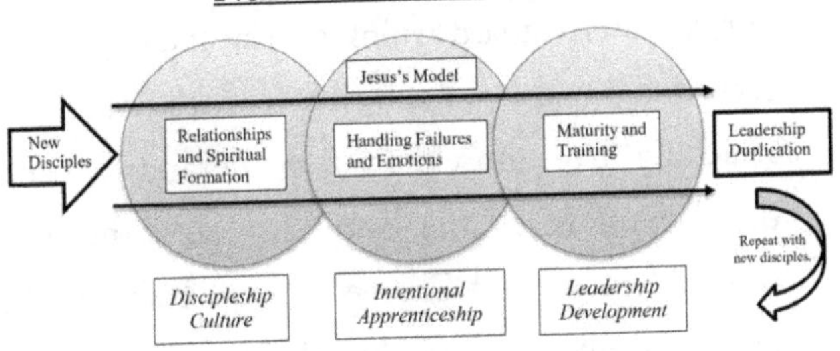

As John Mark began to develop leaders, he used the apprentice model. Oden writes, "Anianus himself began preaching and became Mark's helper and later successor as leader of the Alexandrian Church" (Sawirus, HP, 144–45).[35]

Not only did Mark help develop Anianus into a leader, he also helped develop other disciples into leaders. Oden mentions Sawirus when he says, "He ordained Anianus bishop of Alexandria, and also ordained three priests and seven deacons, and appointed these eleven to serve and to comfort the faithful brethren."[36]

Jerome mentions John Mark's work in developing leaders in the church at Alexandria as well. Needham mentions this in his book when he talks about Jerome's "letter to Evangelus (letter 146)." Jerome writes,

> The apostle [Paul] teaches clearly that presbyters and bishops are identical. . . . When in later times one presbyter was selected as president over the rest, this was to guard against schism and to prevent each individual from splitting Christ's church by attaching it to himself. Even at Alexandria, from the days of Mark the Evangelist until the days when Heraclas and Dionysius were bishops, the presbyters always chose one of their own number as bishop. . . . [37]

Dr. Oden tells of the leadership genealogy of John Mark in Alexandria in *The African Memory of Mark* in the section entitled, "The Heirs of Mark." He indicates this lineage is from the "Martyrium Marci" (The Martyrdom of Mark)[38]:

"Mark's earliest disciples named Anianas/Anianus (AD 68), Milaios/Malchus, Sabinos/Sabinus and Kerdon/Cerdo, following Mark's martyrdom. They presided over the church of Alexandria from AD 68–109, recording forty years of leadership in Egyptian Christianity following Mark's death."[39] What Mark began with Anianus succeeding and other successors to follow, is the very essence of a statement by T.D. Jakes, "Success is not success without a successor."[40]

Oden goes on to write, "Between the eighth year of Nero (A.D. 62) and the tenth year of Commodus (A.D. 189), there were reportedly ten bishops of Alexandria—from Mark to Demetrius, according to highly revered Coptic liturgical celebrations. These were confirmed in Eusebius. What do we know about these earliest Christian leaders on the African continent? They all understood themselves as successors of St. Mark."[41]

In *The African Memory of Mark,* Oden gives a more detailed list on page 172 of the Alexandrian leadership:

> Mark was succeeded by Anianus (62–85), and Anianus by Avilius (85–98), Avilius by Cerdo (98–109), Cerdo by Primus (109–122), and the line then continues as a direct succession: from Primus then Justus(122–130), Eumenes (130–142), Marcianus/Mark II (143–154), Celadion (157–167), Agrippinus (167–180) and Julian (180–189) before you get to the great Demetrius (189–231). They continue to Dionysius (247–264) and on eventually to Athanasius (326–373) and Cyril (412–444).

Dr. Oden goes on to say that this documented lineage of succession has "the implication: Believers could therefore trust that their apostolic teachings were reliably remembered and faithfully transmitted."[42] Some scholars may try to push against this lineage because of the limited evidence available. But, this type of record keeping wasn't only done in Alexandria. It was also done in Rome and Antioch.

As Oden says, "All major centers of Christianity were morally bound to keep records validating their historic succession from the apostles, as we see in Ignatius." But, "the written records were harder to protect in Egypt than in Rome or Antioch."[43]

TIERS OF LEADERSHIP

From this information it appears that Mark intentionally created a culture of leadership development. These leaders are raised up to take the mantle when leaders move off the scene. As leaders, we must create a culture of leadership development within the church so more people can become disciples of Jesus and grow in their faith. But as the church grows, we will need to begin to think not only about discipleship and developing emerging leaders, but also how to develop leaders who will lead other leaders. The church will need leaders of leaders—such as in Mark's case developing Anianus to become the bishop who led other leaders (three priests and seven deacons.)

For example, as the church begins to reach 200 members, the leader must start thinking about how to develop leaders who will lead other leaders. Generally, the leader must begin to think about layers of leadership. In *Designed to Lead*, Geiger and Peck speak to the different levels or layers of leadership. They speak of it as a pipeline (system) for developing leaders. They modified their example from Ram Charan's book *The Leadership Pipeline*[44]:

- Lead Yourself (be in a group)
- Lead Others (lead a group or team)
- Lead Leaders (shepherd or coach a group of leaders)
- Lead Ministries (direct a ministry area)

This same hierarchy of leadership and responsibility is seen in the counsel Jethro gives to Moses in Exodus chapter 18. Jethro tells Moses in verses 21 and 22, "Select from all the people able men, such as fear God, men of truth, hating covetousness; and place such over them to be rulers of thousands, rulers of hundreds, rulers of fifties, and rulers of ten. And let them judge the people at all times. Then it will be that every great matter they shall bring to you, but every small matter they themselves shall judge. So, it will be easier for you, for they will bear the burden with you."

Jethro's counsel to Moses was to establish levels of leadership and responsibilities for leaders within Israel. The leadership levels were:

- Groups of thousands
- Groups of hundreds
- Groups of fifties
- Groups of tens

200 AND BEYOND

Let's go back to the example of the church approaching 200 members. It has been documented by Ed Stetzer and others that as a church moves toward 200 members, the role of the pastor has to change and the church's organizational structure has to change. The pastor has to become more of a specialist focusing on casting vision, clarifying the mission, working on the structures and systems of the church, managing the church's staff, and leadership development.

But at 200 members, the pastor has to think through how to duplicate leaders that will lead other leaders. So those new leaders of leaders can take over some of the areas the pastor was leading. Stetzer suggests looking for eight leaders to develop into leaders of leaders to help you move the congregation past the 200 mark.

This 200 number is not only talked about in church growth material, it is also spoken about in business books. Patrick Lencioni talks about it in his book *The Five Dysfunctions of a Team*. In the book, he tells a fable of a company called Decision Tech who hires a new CEO, Kathryn Peterson, to turn the company around by working with its executive leadership team.

In the book, Lencioni shows the process the CEO moves the team through to become a unified, results-oriented team and organization. At the end of the story, as the company improves and the number of employees grows past 250 people, Lencioni says, "Kathryn decided it was time to trim down the number of executives who reported directly to her. She believed that the larger the company, the smaller the team should be at the top."[45]

While the story is a fable about business, there is some wisdom that can be gleaned for the church. As the church continues to grow, the senior leader/pastor will have to continue adjusting the leadership and organizational structure to allow the church to continue to grow, as well as continue to develop new leaders and leaders of leaders to make sure the growth is healthy, manageable, and sustainable.

At each level, there needs to be training for skills development, coaching for feedback and evaluation, and clear expectations so there is no miscommunication. These layers of leadership and development will have to be developed over time as the church grows. While all churches will not have the same roles and trainings, pastors and churches can learn best practices from other churches who are further along than they are. The leader must continually watch the growth of the church to see when it needs to add another layer of leadership.

MARK'S DEATH

Oden gives multiple accounts of how John Mark died. The first account Oden gives in *The African Memory of Mark* tells of how John Mark was attacked by an angry mob of Alexandrians on Easter.[46] The mob grabbed John Mark and put a noose on his neck and dragged him through the stone streets of Alexandria. "Just as the cross became a symbol of Jesus's self-sacrifice, so did the rope with horses become the symbol of Mark's sacrifice. A dragging death was intended to be a slow and torturous death."[47]

The story goes on to say, because John Mark did not die while being dragged, "Mark was thrown in prison half alive."[48] We are told, "Mark was dragged again over the cobbled roads of Alexandria, his body battered, this time dragged to his death. The mob was determined to torture him again before his death. He was dragged back to the Serapeum. His blood was spilt on the streets of Alexandria until he at last died a tortured martyr's death. His blood attested the blood of the Son of God."[49]

"Amid the confusion, faithful believers removed the body of the saint and secretly buried him. . . . The burial site was the same cow pasture (boukolos) where Mark had first nurtured the worshiping community following his meeting with Anianus."[50]

"Mark, then, according to African memory . . . was martyred in A.D. 68."[51]

Oden gives another account of John Mark's death from the Roman martyrology which summarizes the life of John Mark. He writes, "The Roman martyrology similarly summarizes the martyrdom of Mark as a disciple and interpreter of Peter. It reports that Mark was born in Africa, wrote the Gospel of Mark in Rome, preached in Egypt, established the church in Alexandria, where he was imprisoned and suffered, and was comforted by an angel. In prison the Lord himself appeared to Mark to call him to his celestial home. This happened in the eighth year of Nero (*Vetus martyrologium romanum*, April 25)."[52]

While these accounts do not agree on how Mark died, they do agree on where he died. Which is the city of Alexandria.

MARK'S LEGACY

Mark became an example in Africa of a faithful witness to what it meant to follow Christ, to preach the Gospel of Jesus, and to give one's life for King Jesus. There are many in Africa who followed his example of Christian martyrdom[53]:

- The martyrs of Scilli (7/17/180)—Seven men and five women murdered.
- Perpetua—First known Christian martyr. A pregnant woman martyred for her faith in Jesus.[54]
- The martyrs of Mauretania, Nubia, and Lybia
- Origen's father, Leonides
- Peter of Alexandria
- Catherine of Alexandria
- Cyprian of Carthage

There are also many historical Christian thinkers in Africa who stand on the shoulders of John Mark:

- Clement of Alexandria
- Origin
- Athanasius
- Cyril
- Tertullian
- Augustine
- Cyprian of Carthage
- Pachomius—Contributed to history of prayer and holy living.[55]

God was able to accomplish all of this through a man, who most people would have viewed as a screwup. Dr. Wiersbe gives a resounding endorsement of the life, ministry, and leadership of John Mark. He writes, "John Mark is an encouragement to everyone who has failed in his first attempt to serve God. He did not sit around and sulk. He got back into the ministry and proved himself faithful to the Lord and to the apostle Paul. He was one of the men who stayed."[56]

TOGETHER IS BETTER

From the legacy of John Mark, we are able to see how he helped to develop a culture of discipleship and leadership in Alexandria. If we desire to impact future generations of Christian leaders, we must do the same.

We must concentrate on discipleship and leadership. We cannot separate the two. In the church, leaders must be disciples of Jesus and all disciples should have an opportunity to lead in some capacity within the local church if they are willing and able. Whether it's leading someone to Christ, a one-on-one Bible study, a Bible study class, or a ministry within the local church.

Eric Geiger and Kevin Peck said in their book *Designed to Lead*, "Divorcing leadership development from discipleship can leave people more skilled and less sanctified. And when competency and skill outpace character, leaders are set up for a fall. We don't serve people well if we teach them how to lead without teaching them how to follow Him. We don't serve leaders well if we develop their skills without shepherding their character."[57]

In order to make sure we are focusing on discipleship and leadership, we must create, examine, readjust, and sometimes make changes within our churches. We must work on developing healthy cultures that will produce disciples and leaders. Geiger and Peck say, "Healthy church cultures are conducive for leadership development. . . . A church's culture has the power to significantly impede or empower its effectiveness in the Great Commission and the call to multiplication."[58]

BEING REMEMBERED

When you move on to heaven to be with Jesus, what do you want to be remembered for? What legacy do you want to leave behind? Peter Drucker speaks on this in the book *Management* in the chapter on Revitalizing Oneself. In the chapter, he gives his seven personal experiences. The last experience, "what to be remembered for," is very useful. Under that experience he gives three things he has learned which is helpful for us as we think about our legacy:[59]

- First, one has to ask oneself what one wants to be remembered for.
- Second, that should change as one gets older. It should change with one's own maturity and with the changes in the world.
- Finally, one thing worth being remembered for is the difference one makes in the lives of people.

CONNECTING LEGACIES

Before we close this chapter, let's revisit Richard Allen's legacy. Allen loving on his community in preaching and serving, is connected with the legacy of John Wesley, the founder of Methodism. John

Wesley was ordained as a priest in the Church of England in 1728. Wesley and his brother Charles had a group of Bible students who diligently studied the Scriptures, attended worship services, and visited the Oxford prisoners. They became known as Methodist because of their methodical approach to studying the Scriptures and life. Eventually the Methodists broke away from the Church of England.

Not only was Wesley a formidable church leader, he was also against slavery, and a student of church history. In the late 1730s, the Wesley brothers visited the British colony, Georgia, in North America where John Wesley saw the horrid experience of American slavery. John Wesley would refer to the slave trade in general as the "execrable sum of all villainies."[60] But in a letter to William Wilberforce, he called "American slavery (the vilest that ever saw the sun)."[61] In 1774, he wrote a tract called *Thoughts on Slavery* where "he attacked the Slave Trade and the slave traders . . . and proposed a boycott of slave-produced sugar and rum."[62]

Wesley also preached against slavery. He said about slavery, "Give liberty to who liberty is due, that is to every child of men, to every partaker of human nature. Let none serve you but by his own act and deed, by his own voluntary action. Away with all whips, all chains, all compulsion. Be gentle toward all men; and see that you invariably do with everyone as you would he should do unto you."[63]

When you read John Wesley's writings you find out that he was also a church historian, studying the early church. In particular, some of his most revered early church leaders were from the continent of Africa. The Apostolic church fathers of Tertullian, Origen, Clement of Alexandria, Cyprian, and Athanasius greatly influenced him.

Thomas Oden recites the words of John Wesley in *The Rebirth of African Orthodoxy* where Wesley writes, speaking of these church leaders as "the most authentic commentators on Scripture, as being both nearest the fountain, and eminently endued with the Spirit by whom all Scripture was given. . . . "[64] Oden goes on to write, "Wesley thought that these early African teachers were especially helpful in "the explication of a doctrine that is not sufficiently explained, or for confirmation of a doctrine received."[65]

Wesley not only studied these giants who stand on the shoulders of John Mark, he also encourages others to do so. He writes how they had "the advantage of living in the apostolic times, of hearing the holy Apostles and conversing with them."[66] Therefore,

Christians "cannot with any reason doubt of what they deliver . . . but ought to receive it, though not with equal veneration, yet with only little less regard than we do the sacred writings of those who were their masters and instructors . . . as worthy of a much greater respect than any composures which have been made since."[67]

Now we come full circle. We see Richard Allen's legacy is connected to the legacy of John Wesley. And Wesley's legacy is connected to the legacy and teachings of many of the leading African teachers of the second and third centuries. And their legacy is connected to the legacy of John Mark. The legacy we leave behind matters.

EXERCISE:

1. The Legacy Question: How do you want to be remembered as a spiritual leader?

   ____

   ____

   ____

2. What evangelism method will your church teach so disciples can learn how to share the Gospel of Jesus?

   ____

   ____

   ____

3. What catechism process will your church use to help disciples grow in their faith?

   ____

   ____

   ____

4. What systems must you create to develop leaders of leaders?

   ____

   ____

   ____

NOTES:

CHAPTER 7: FINAL THOUGHTS

"Success is not a matter of mastering subtle, sophisticated theory, but rather of embracing common sense with uncommon levels of discipline and persistence." [1]

Patrick Lencioni

As we conclude our time together, I would like to speak a word to aspiring leaders about the importance of self-development. As I thought about how to close this book, my mind went to the many challenges Frederick Douglass wrote about in the narrative of his life. Douglass, named Frederick Augustus Washington Bailey, was born sometime around the year of 1818 in Tuckahoe, Maryland as an American slave.

In the Afterword of the *Narrative of the Life of Frederick Douglass*, Gregory Stephens writes how Frederick Douglass became a cultural hero, and mentions how Michael Lind wrote in his book *The Next American Nation* that Douglass is "the greatest American, who deserves a monument.[2] . . . He is a great American precisely because he was part of social movements that transcended the barrier of 'race,' religion, gender, and nation. More than any other public figure in the nineteenth century, he challenged us to expand our definitions of self, community, and nation."[3]

Douglass didn't start out being a hero, though. He was born into chattel slavery and was known as a mulatto because his mother was black and his father was white. There were rumors that his father was his slave master, but he could not confirm those rumors. He believed it could have been very possible because it was common practice for slave owners to father children with slave women so they could have more slaves. Therefore, enslaving their own children.

Even though Douglass was born a slave, he said about his childhood: "From earliest recollection, I date the entertainment of a deep conviction that slavery would not always be able to hold me in its foul embrace; and in the darkest hours of my career in slavery, this living word of faith and spirit of hope departed not from me, but remained like ministering angels to cheer me through the gloom. This good spirit was from God, and to him I offer thanksgiving and praise."[4]

Douglass was alive during a time when it was illegal to teach slaves to read. But when he was sent to Baltimore to be the slave of Mr. and Mrs. Auld as a boy, his spark for freedom was lit through education. Mrs. Auld began teaching Douglass the ABC's and how to spell words. When Mr. Auld found out, he was furious and told his wife to stop teaching him.

He told his wife, "Learning will spoil the best nigger in the world. Now . . . if you teach that nigger how to read, there would be no keeping him. It would forever unfit him to be a slave. He would at once become unmanageable, and of no value to his master. As to himself, it could do him no good, but a great deal of harm. It would make him discontented and unhappy."[5] Douglass writes, "From that moment, I understood the pathway from slavery to freedom. . . . Though conscious of the difficulty of learning without a teacher, I set out with high hope, and a fixed purpose, at whatever cost of trouble, to learn how to read."[6]

At about twelve years old, Douglass devised a plan of turning the little white boys in his community into his teachers. Even though he was a slave, he was given more than enough food to eat so he would take food to some of the poor white boys to befriend them. He writes, "This bread I used to bestow upon the hungry little urchins, who, in return, would give me that more valuable bread of knowledge."[7]

After learning how to read, Frederick Douglass set his pursuit to learning how to write because as he said in his book, "I might have occasion to write my own pass."[8] He began learning how to write letters while laboring at a shipyard. He saw ship carpenters writing letters on pieces of timber and he began to copy their writing. Then when he met a boy on the street, he would challenge him to a writing contest. He would also copy the 'Italics' [letters]in Webster's Spelling Book."[9] He would also take the old copy books that his master's son had completed in school and write in them until he learned how to write.

Eventually Douglass was sent from Baltimore to St. Michael's, Maryland. In his teenage years Douglass truly felt the harshness of slavery, lacking food, being beaten, and the uncertainty about life. One day at the age of sixteen, after being beaten severely by his master, Douglass would begin to literally fight back when he was getting beaten. He writes, "I did not hesitate to let it be known of me, that the white man who expected to succeed in whipping, must also succeed in killing me. From this time I was never again what might be called fairly whipped, though I remained a slave four years afterwards. I had several fights, but was never whipped."[10]

Douglass would eventually begin to teach other slaves how to read. He would teach them how to read in Sabbath School (Sunday school class). He taught slaves on his farm and from neighboring farms how to read. He was teaching them how "to read the will of God" (Bible). The slaves had to keep this Sabbath School under the radar of the slaveowners because if they found out, they would shut it down—of which they eventually did. At one point, Douglass had over forty pupils in his school, all of which were his fellow slaves. Many of them learned how to read under Douglass's teaching.

Douglass wrote, "Every moment they spent in that school, they were liable to be taken up, and given thirty-nine lashes. They came because they wished to learn. Their minds had been starved by their cruel masters. They had been shut up in mental darkness. I taught them, because it was the delight of my soul to be doing something that looked like bettering the condition of my race."[11]

After this experience, Douglass was determined to escape to freedom. He initially tried to escape with some of the slaves from his Sabbath School, but someone told the slaveowners of the plan and they were put in jail. When Douglass's owner got him out of jail, he sent him back to Baltimore with his master's brother Hugh. His master Hugh began to hire him out as a laborer and then took Douglass's paycheck.

On September 3, 1838, Douglass ran away to New York, a free state. While in New York, he met Mr. David Ruggles. Mr. Ruggles helped fugitive slaves successfully escape the wickedness of slavery. With the assistance of Mr. David Ruggles, Douglass, along with his new bride Anna, left New York and moved to New Bedford, Massachusetts. When they arrived in New Bedford, they met Mr. and Mrs. Johnson who help them establish themselves in this new city. It was Mr. Johnson who suggested Frederick take the last name Douglass. For three years he worked any kind of job he could find to take care of his bride and himself. He got involved in the anti-slavery world and began publicly speaking out against the wickedness of slavery in America and Europe.

From the life of Frederick Douglass, I want to share some thoughts.

First: Develop a passion for reading. For many people, reading can be challenging and boring. But the more you read, the better you get at it. To help with the boredom, read things you are passionate about—such as developing your character, your leadership, and your craft. Also, the more you read, you will begin to enjoy it more. I used to hate reading; but as I read more, I enjoyed it more.

Second: Develop the art of writing. This habit does a few things for you. First, writing helps you get clarity of thought. You're able to put on paper all of the ideas and concepts you have floating around in your mind. Next, learning how to write well can help you share your ideas with people who you may never meet because they can read your work. Finally, writing may help you "write your own pass." God may use your writing to open doors for you that you never knew were possible. God has used my books to get me speaking engagements, workshop opportunities, and to meet new people.

Third: Don't allow yourself to become a victim of circumstances. Develop perseverance and tenacity. Don't allow hardships and difficulties to stop you from learning and growing. Life can be hard, but the God you serve is more powerful than anything you or I will ever face. I refuse to roll over and die because life is hard. Life experiences may beat me up, but my God will help me get up and continue to fight on for his glory.

Fourth: Look for ways to teach and empower others. Do not hold on to the knowledge you have. Learn to be a giver of information and to help others advance. Not only will it bless and encourage your soul, you'll better understand what you're teaching. You will grow more in the process as well. Please realize God opens doors for people who have a heart to serve and help others get better. I truly believe all those years God allowed me to teach Sunday school before I became a pastor, prepared me to become a more capable and competent Bible teacher.

Fifth: Look for open doors from God for advancement. God can open a door for you to advance anytime he wants. One of the ways the Lord speaks to us is through our circumstances and situations. Stay attuned to the Holy Spirit's prompting and guidance by prayerfully considering the options the Lord is placing before you. When the coronavirus (COVID -19) pandemic caused the state of Ohio to shut down, God used that situation to allow me time to figure out how we can be more intentional about disciple making and leadership development. During the pandemic, I was able to write the book you just finished reading so Mt. Calvary and I can get more clarity for our ministry.

Sixth: Value the relationships God has sent into your life. Do not take relationships lightly. God sends people into your life for a reason. Learn what you can from people. Value and respect them. And watch God work through them.

Listen, learn from Frederick Douglass. Don't allow setbacks, hardship, and obstacles stop you from becoming the person and leader God is calling you to become. Continue to trust God, pursue leadership, and keep growing. God has a plan for your life. While you may be wondering when the Lord is going to elevate you, stay patient and work on your character and your competence.

Try your best to learn from your mistakes and from godly leaders. Be open to feedback, correction, and guidance with humility and joy. Do your best in your current role and learn as much as you can where you are about how the organization works.

If the Lord graces your life with a mentor, keep the acrostic "FAITH" in mind. This comes from the book *Mentoring* by Tim Elmore.[12] This acrostic shows the behavior mentors are looking for in mentees.

F Faith: Be faithful to your commitments and to the Christian faith.

A Available: Make time to learn, work, and for opportunities.

I Initiative: Try new things without be asked to do them.

T Teachable: Being open to learn and not being a know-it-all.

H Hungry: Passionate about God, ministry, vocation, and growth.

If you take time to cultivate these things, watch what God will do in you and through you.

If you're looking for a mentor and God has not sent one yet, begin being mentored through reading books and attending conferences and workshops by people you admire and respect. If you don't have any extra money to do those things, the internet is available. Listen and watch their podcasts, lectures, sermons, and trainings. Go to their websites and feast, learn, and grow.

I have been mentored through the years by people like Myles Munroe, John Maxwell, Michael Gerber, T.D. Jakes, and many others—and I have never met any of them personally. Don't let not having a mentor in life stop you from growing and becoming the next leader.

God Bless and stay on the journey.

NOTES:

APPENDIX

MOUNT CALVARY BAPTIST CHURCH
LEADERSHIP HONOR CODE

"Follow my example, as I follow the example of Christ."

1 Corinthians 11:1 (NIV)

As an essential part of the Mount Calvary Leadership family, you have a responsibility to develop and exhibit mature Christian behavior. This should be the basic premise of your desire to work in a Servant/Leader position here at Mount Calvary.

I commit myself to Mount Calvary Baptist by regularly attending church services, praying for church leaders and church needs, speaking only life-giving words about the church and its leaders, and giving my tithes and offerings.

I will give attention to the development of relationships with other believers, be a team player, and cultivate unity with the church.

I will keep myself accountable to the people in church authority over me.

I will lead and serve my ministry team with humility and honor.

I will keep my word, not gossip, not criticize, not complain, and will not repeat information given to me in confidence unless the information is causing harm to the individual or another person.

Even if my personal convictions differ, I will publicly abstain from profanity, smoking, much alcoholic beverages, illegal drugs, and all behavior which could influence a weaker Christian to fall away from his or her faith.

I will strive to demonstrate biblical standards in all situations in church, as well as outside church activities.

I will encourage others to grow in Christ and to become Servants/Leaders themselves.

I will faithfully attend Monthly Leadership meetings and Bible Study.

In keeping the Honor Code, I understand that I am not being restricted, but liberated to know true joy and peace that Christ purchased for me at the cross.

Name:____________________ Date:______________

Mt. Calvary's Discipleship Process

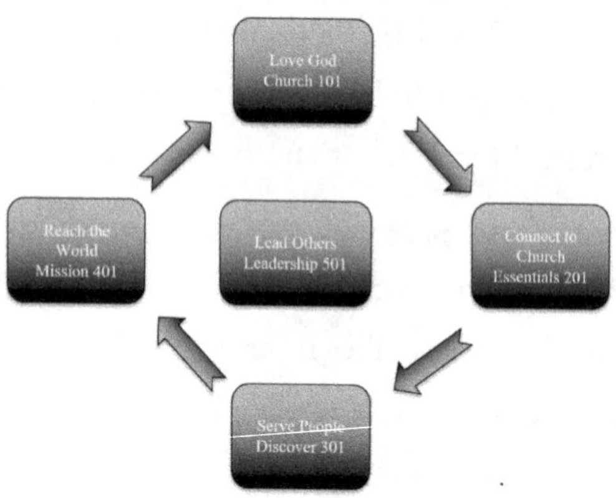

Based off the Great Commandment (Matt. 22:37-40) and the Great Commission (Matt. 28:28-20) we have a 5-step discipleship process. Each step is connected to a class in Mount Calvary's Growth Track.

1. **Love** God – "all your heart all your soul, and all your mind" (Worship – Church 101)
2. ***Connect*** to Church – *"Teach … to obey all commands"* (Fellowship – Essentials 201)
3. ***Serve*** People – *"Love your neighbor as yourself"* (Ministry – Discovery 301)
4. ***Reach*** the World – *"Go…make disciples"* (Evangelism – Mission 401)
5. ***Lead*** Others – *"Take heed therefore unto yourselves, and to all the flock, over the which the Holy Ghost hath made you overseers"* – Acts 20:28 KJV (Mentoring – Leadership 501)

ENDNOTES

Chapter 1

1. John Maxwell quote. https://www.inc.com/peter-economy/44-inspiring-john-c-maxwell-quotes-that-will-take-you-to-leadership-success.html.
2. Thomas C. Oden, *The African Memory of Mark* (Downer Grove: InterVarsity, 2011), 52.
3. Ibid., 52-53.
4. Ibid., 36.
5. Ibid., 170.
6. Barna Group, *The State of Pastors Report.* A Barna Report Produced in partnership with Pepperdine University (2017), 86.
7. Barna Group, *The Connected Generation.* A Barna Report produced in partnership with World Vision (2019), 28.
8. Ibid., 38.

Chapter 2

1. Erwin Raphael McManus, *An Unstoppable Force* (Colorado Springs: David C. Cook, 2001), 21.
2. https://homeboyindustries.org/our-story/about-homeboy/
3. Thomas C. Oden, *The African Memory of Mark* (Downer Grove: InterVarsity, 2011), 21.
4. *Holman Study Bible,* NKJV Edition (Nashville: Holman Bible Publishers, 2013), 1656.

5. Ibid., 1656.

6. Thomas C. Oden, *The African Memory of Mark* (Downer Grove: InterVarsity, 2011). 22.

7. Ibid., 23.

8. *The New Interpreter's Bible Volume X* (Nashville: Abingdon Press, 2002), 180.

9. F. F. Bruce, *The Book of the* Acts (Grand Rapids: WM. B. Eerdmans Publishing Company, 1971), 251.

10. Bruce B. Barton, Linda K. Taylor, J. Richard Love, Len Woods, and David R. Veerman, *Life Application Bible Commentary: Acts* (Carol Stream: Tyndale House Publishers, Inc., 1993), 208.

11. F. F. Bruce, *The Pauline Circle* (E-book) (Nashville: Kingsley Books, 2017).

12. F. F. Bruce, *The Pauline Circle* (E-book) (Nashville: Kingsley Books, 2017).

13. Aubrey Malphurs and Will Mancini, *Building Leaders* (Grand Rapids: Baker Books, 2004), 34.

14. Ibid., 190.

15. Ed Stetzer and Daniel Im, *Planting Missional Churches* (Nashville: B&H Publishing Group, 2016), 292.

16. Ibid., 292.

17. Jeff Christopherson and Mac Lake, *Kingdom First* (Nashville: B&H Publishing Group, 2015), 200.

18. Ed Stetzer and Daniel Im, *Planting Missional Churches* (Nashville: B&H Publishing Group, 2016), 207.

19. Jeff Christopherson and Mac Lake, *Kingdom First* (Nashville: B&H Publishing Group, 2015), 202.

Chapter 3

1. The Walt Disney Story. https://www.youtube.com/watch?v=dtV2Ilr3Fk4
2. http://www.kansascitycomics.com/?page_id=1558
3. https://www.britannica.com/biography/Walt-Disney
4. The Walt Disney Story. https://www.youtube.com/watch?v=dtV2Ilr3Fk4
5. Ram Charan, *Leaders at All Levels* (San Francisco: Jossey-Bass, 2007), 25.
6. F. F. Bruce, *The Book of the* Acts (Grand Rapids: WM. B. Eerdmans Publishing Company, 1971), 257.
7. Warren W. Wiersbe, *The Wiersbe Bible Commentary: New Testament* (Colorado Springs: David C. Cook, 2007), 364.
8. F. F. Bruce, *The Book of the* Acts (Grand Rapids: WM. B. Eerdmans Publishing Company, 1971), 258.
9. F. F. Bruce, *The Pauline Circle* (E-book) (Nashville: Kingsley Books, 2017).
10. F. F. Bruce, *The Pauline Circle* (E-book) (Nashville: Kingsley Books, 2017).
11. Thomas C. Oden, *The African Memory of Mark* (Downer Grove: InterVarsity, 2011), 87.
12. Jeff Iorg, *The Case for Antioch* (Nashville: B&H Publishing Group, 2011), 13.
13. Ibid., 20.
14. Ibid., 14.
15. Ibid., 15.

16. Ibid., 15.
17. Dave Ferguson and Jon Ferguson, *Exponential* (Grand Rapids: Zondervan, 2010), 33.
18. Thomas C. Oden, *The African Memory of Mark* (Downer Grove: InterVarsity, 2011), 21.
19. John C. Maxwell, *Developing the Leader Within You* (Nashville: Thomas Nelson, Inc., 1993), 132.
20. F. F. Bruce, *The Book of the* Acts (Grand Rapids: WM. B. Eerdmans Publishing Company, 1971), 266.

Chapter 4

1. Peter F. Drucker and Joseph A. Maciariello, *Management, Revised Edition* (New York: HarperCollins,2008), 251.
2. https://www.forbes.com/sites/sorensonimpact/2020/02/04/higher-hope-lower-recidivism-for-defys-eits/#5123df175c5c
3. Devyventures.com.
4. Warren W. Wiersbe, *The Wiersbe Bible Commentary: New Testament* (Colorado Springs: David C. Cook, 2007), 365.
5. Reggie McNeal, *Practicing Greatness* (San Francisco: Jossey-Bass, 2006), 76
6. Ibid., 76-80.
7. Warren W. Wiersbe, *The Wiersbe Bible Commentary: New Testament* (Colorado Springs: David C. Cook, 2007), 372.
8. Dave Browning, *Deliberate Simplicity* (Grand Rapids: Zondervan, 2009), 58.

9. Peter Scazzero, *Emotionally Healthy Spirituality* (Grand Rapids: Zondervan, 2006), 17.
10. Ibid., 143-144.
11. Ibid., 175.
12. Ibid., 179-180.
13. Ibid., 178.
14. Ibid., 184.
15. Ibid., 184.
16. Ibid., 185.
17. Ibid., 187.
18. Ibid., 187.
19. Ibid., 188.
20. Jeff Iorg, *The Case for Antioch* (Nashville: B&H Publishing Group, 2011), 117.
21. Ibid., 117.
22. Ibid., 128-134.
23. Ibid., 130.
24. Ibid., 130.
25. Ibid., 131.
26. Ibid., 131-132.
27. Ibid., 132.
28. Ibid., 133.
29. Ibid., 133.
30. Ibid., 134.

Chapter 5

1. Albert Einstein (Quote) https://www.inc.com/jayson-demers/35-quotes-about-perseverance-and-never-giving-up.html
2. James C. Collins and Jerry I. Porras, *Built to Last* (New York: HarperBusiness, 1997), 158.
3. Ibid., 151.
4. Ibid., 152.
5. Ibid., 155.
6. Aubrey Malphurs and Will Mancini, *Building Leaders* (Grand Rapids: Baker Books, 2004), 146.
7. Ibid., 146.
8. Eric Geiger and Kevin Peck, *Designed to Lead* (Nashville: B&H Publishing Group, 2016), 177.
9. Warren W. Wiersbe, *The Wiersbe Bible Commentary: New Testament* (Colorado Springs: David C. Cook, 2007), 696.
10. Bruce B. Barton, Mark Fackler, Linda Chaffee Taylor, and David R. Veerman, *Life Application Bible Commentary: 1 & 2 Peter / Jude* (Carol Stream: Tyndale House Publishers, Inc., 1993), 140.
11. *compiled by Felix Just, S.J., Ph.D,* Early Christian Texts Quoted by Eusebius on the Authorship of the Gospels and the Book of Revelation. http://catholic-resources.org/Bible/Eusebius_Gospels.htm
12. Thomas C. Oden, *The African Memory of Mark* (Downer Grove: InterVarsity, 2011), 191.

13. Gospel of Mark: External evidence regarding the authorship of Mark's Gospel http://ntresources.com/blog/?p=300

14. Thomas C. Oden, *The African Memory of Mark* (Downer Grove: InterVarsity, 2011), 195.

15. Ibid., 191.

16. Gospel of Mark: External evidence regarding the authorship of Mark's Gospel http://ntresources.com/blog/?p=300

17. Gospel of Mark: External evidence regarding the authorship of Mark's Gospel http://ntresources.com/blog/?p=300

18. *Holman Study Bible*, NKJV Edition (Nashville: Holman Bible Publishers, 2013), 1656.

19. Peter F. Drucker and Joseph A. Maciariello, *Management, Revised Edition* (New York: HarperCollins,2008), 254.

20. Ibid., 255.

21. Ibid., 256.

22. Ibid., 256.

23. Malphurs and Will Mancini, *Building Leaders* (Grand Rapids: Baker Books, 2004), 184-186.

24. Ibid., 186.

Chapter 6

1. Eric Geiger and Kevin Peck, *Designed to Lead* (Nashville: B&H Publishing Group, 2016), 103.

2. PBS IdeaStream, Richard Allen Article, https://www.pbs.org/wgbh/aia/part3/3p97.html

3. A&E Television Networks, Richard Allen Biography, https://www.biography.com/religious-figure/richard-allen

4. Christianity Today, Richard Allen Article

https://www.christianitytoday.com/history/people/denominationalfounders/richard-allen.html

5. PBS IdeaStream, Richard Allen Article, https://www.pbs.org/wgbh/aia/part3/3p97.html

6. PBS IdeaStream, Richard Allen Article, https://www.pbs.org/wgbh/aia/part3/3p97.html

7. A&E Television Networks, Richard Allen Biography, https://www.biography.com/religious-figure/richard-allen

8. Jemar Tisby, *The Color of Compromise* (Grand Rapids, Zondervan Reflective, 2019), 54.

9. A&E Television Networks, Richard Allen Biography, https://www.biography.com/religious-figure/richard-allen

10. A&E Television Networks, Richard Allen Biography, https://www.biography.com/religious-figure/richard-allen

11. Bruce B. Barton, Mark Fackler, Linda Chaffee Taylor, and David R. Veerman, *Life Application Bible Commentary: 1 & 2 Timothy and Titus* (Carol Stream: Tyndale House Publishers, Inc., 1993), 223.

12. Thomas C. Oden, *The African Memory of Mark* (Downer Grove: InterVarsity, 2011), 138.

13. Ibid., 174.

14. Ibid.
15. Ibid., 33.
16. Ibid., 177.
17. Nick Needham, *2000 Years of Christ's Power Volume 1* (Scotland: Christian Focus Publications Ltd, 2016), 127.
18. Thomas C. Oden, *The African Memory of Mark* (Downer Grove: InterVarsity, 2011), 143.
19. Ibid., 64.
20. Ibid., 65.
21. Ibid., 66.
22. Ibid., 61.
23. Ibid., 145.
24. Ibid., 146.
25. Ibid., 147.
26. Ibid., 147.
27. Ibid., 148.
28. Ibid., 148.
29. Ibid., 241.
30. Ibid., 242.
31. Ibid., 241.
32. Ibid., 244.
33. Jeff Iorg, *The Case for Antioch* (Nashville: B&H Publishing Group, 2011), 91-92.
34. Jim Putman, *Real-Life Discipleship* (Colorado Springs: NavPress, 2010) (E-book).

35. Thomas C. Oden, *The African Memory of Mark* (Downner Grove: InterVarsity, 2011), 148.
36. Ibid., 149.
37. Nick Needham, *2000 Years of Christ's Power Volume 1* (Scotland: Christian Focus Publications Ltd, 2016), 69.
38. Thomas C. Oden, *The African Memory of Mark* (Downner Grove: InterVarsity, 2011), 169.
39. Ibid., 169-170.
40. https://www.goodreads.com/author/quotes/72902.T_D_Jakes?page=4
41. Ibid., 171.
42. Ibid., 172.
43. Ibid., 170.
44. Eric Geiger and Kevin Peck, *Designed to Lead* (Nashville: B&H Publishing Group, 2016), 186-187.
45. Patrick Lencioni, *The Five Dysfunctions of a Team* (San Francisco: Jossey-Bass, 2002), 182.
46. Thomas C. Oden, *The African Memory of Mark* (Downner Grove: InterVarsity, 2011), 153.
47. Ibid., 154.
48. Ibid., 156.
49. Ibid., 157.
50. Ibid., 158.
51. Ibid., 35.
52. Ibid., 65.
53. Ibid., 170.

54. Ibid., 31.

55. Ibid., 31.

56. Warren W. Wiersbe, *The Wiersbe Bible Commentary: New Testament* (Colorado Springs: David C. Cook, 2007), 696.

57. Eric Geiger and Kevin Peck, *Designed to Lead* (Nashville: B&H Publishing Group, 2016), 160.

58. Ibid., 124.

59. Peter F. Drucker and Joseph A. Maciariello, *Management, Revised Edition* (New York: HarperCollins,2008), 511-512.

60. Christian History Institute, Wesley to Wilberforce Article, https://christianhistoryinstitute.org/magazine/article/wesley-to-wilberforce

61. Christian History Institute, Wesley to Wilberforce Article, https://christianhistoryinstitute.org/magazine/article/wesley-to-wilberforce

62. The Abolition Project, John Wesley Article, http://abolition.e2bn.org/people_32.html

63. The Abolition Project, John Wesley Article, http://abolition.e2bn.org/people_32.html

64. Thomas C. Oden, *The Rebirth of African Orthodoxy*, (Nashville: Abingdon Press, 2016), 16.

65. Ibid., 16.

66. Ibid., 17.

67. Ibid., 17.

Chapter 7—Final Thoughts

1. Patrick Lencioni, *The Five Dysfunctions of a Team* (San Francisco: Jossey-Bass, 2002), 220.
2. Frederick Douglas, *Narrative of the Life of Frederick Douglas* (New York: New American Library, 1997), 129.
3. Ibid., 129-130.
4. Ibid., 46.
5. Ibid., 48.
6. Ibid., 48-49.
7. Ibid., 53.
8. Ibid., 56.
9. Ibid., 57.
10. Ibid., 82-83.
11. Ibid., 90.
12. Tim Elmore, *Mentoring* (Atlanta: Equip and Emerging Young Leaders, 1998), 60.

BIBLIOGRAPHY

Barna Group. *The Connected Generation*. A Barna Report produced in partnership with World Vision: 2019.

Barna Group. *The State of Pastors Report*. A Barna Report Produced in partnership with Pepperdine University: 2017.

Barton, Bruce B., Mark Fackler, Linda Chaffee Taylor, and David R. Veerman. *Life Application Bible Commentary: 1 & 2 Peter/ Jude*. Carol Stream: Tyndale House Publishers, Inc., 1993.

Barton, Bruce B., Linda K. Taylor, J. Richard Love, Len Woods, and David R. Veerman. *Life Application Bible Commentary: Acts*. Carol Stream: Tyndale House Publishers, Inc., 1993.

Blanchard, Kenneth, Ph.D., and Spencer Johnson, M.D. *The One Minute Manager*. New York: The Berkley Publishing Group, 1982.

Browning, Dave. *Deliberate Simplicity*. Grand Rapids: Zondervan, 2009.

Bruce, F. F. *The Book of the* Acts. Grand Rapids: WM. B. Eerdmans Publishing Company, 1971.

Bruce, F. F. *The Pauline Circle,* (E-book). Nashville: Kingsley Books, 2017.

Charan, Ram. *Leaders at All Levels.* San Francisco: Jossey-Bass, 2007.

Christopherson, Jeff, and Mac Lake. *Kingdom First.* Nashville: B&H Publishing Group, 2015.

Collins, James C., and Jerry I. Porras. *Built to Last.* New York: Harper Business, 1997.

Drucker, Peter F., and Joseph A. Maciariello. *Management, Revised Edition.* New York: HarperCollins, 2008.

Elmore, Tim. *Mentoring.* Atlanta: Equip and Emerging Young Leaders, 1998.

Ferguson, Dave, and Jon Ferguson. *Exponential.* Grand Rapids: Zondervan, 2010.

Geiger, Eric, and Kevin Peck. *Designed to Lead.* Nashville: B&H Publishing Group, 2016.

Holman Study Bible, NKJV Edition. Nashville: Holman Bible Publishers, 2013.

Iorg, Jeff. *The Case for Antioch.* Nashville: B&H Publishing Group, 2011.

Lencioni, Patrick. *The Five Dysfunctions of a Team.* San Francisco: Jossey-Bass, 2002.

Malphurs, Aubrey, and Will Mancini. *Building Leaders.* Grand Rapids: Baker Books, 2004.

Mancini, Will. *Church Unique.* San Francisco: Jossey-Bass, 2008.

Marshall, Colin, and Tony Payne. *The Trellis and The Vine.* St. Matthias Press Ltd., 2009.

Maxwell, John C. *Developing the Leader Within You.* Nashville: Thomas Nelson, Inc., 1993.

McManus, Erwin Raphael. *An Unstoppable Force.* Colorado Springs: David C. Cook, 2001.

McNeal, Reggie. *Practicing Greatness.* San Francisco: Jossey-Bass, 2006.

Needham, Nick. *2000 Years of Christ's Power Volume 1.* Scotland: Christian Focus Publications Ltd, 2016.

Oden, Thomas C. *The African Memory of Mark.* Downer Grove: InterVarsity, 2011.

Oden, Thomas C. *The Rebirth of African Orthodoxy.* Nashville: Abingdon Press, 2016.

Putman, Jim. *Real-Life Discipleship.* Colorado Springs: NavPress, 2010.

Rainer, Thom S., and Eric Geiger. *Simple Church.* Nashville: Broadman & Holman Publishers, 2006.

Scazzero, Peter. *Emotionally Healthy Spirituality.* Grand Rapids: Zondervan, 2006.

Stetzer, Ed, and Daniel Im. *Planting Missional Churches.* Nashville: B&H Publishing Group, 2016.

The New Interpreter's Bible. Volume X. Nashville: Abingdon Press, 2002.

Tisby, Jemar. *The Color of Compromise.* Grand Rapids, Zondervan Reflective, 2019.

Wiersbe, Warren W. *The Wiersbe Bible Commentary: New Testament.* Colorado Springs: David C. Cook, 2007

CPSIA information can be obtained
at www.ICGtesting.com
Printed in the USA
BVHW080301280821
615416BV00012B/1113

9 780982 462270